W9-ADQ-000

WITHDRAWN
LENOIR-RHYNE UNIVERSITY

DATE DUE			
Sep 19 68			
Apr 8 '70			
Apr 21 '70			
Mar 6 '73			
GAYLORD			PRINTED IN U.S.A.

Exploring with Polymer

Exploring with Polymer

A GUIDE TO NEW MEDIA FOR YOUNG ADULTS

George Chavatel

 Reinhold Publishing Corporation/New York

CARL A. RUDISILL LIBRARY
LENOIR RHYNE COLLEGE

©1966 by Reinhold Publishing Corporation
All rights reserved
Printed in the United States of America
Library of Congress Catalog Card No. 66-11935

Designed by Prim Diefenderfer
Type set by Graphic Arts Typographers, Inc.
Printed by Port City Press, Inc.
Bound by William Marley Company
Published by Reinhold Publishing Corporation
430 Park Avenue, New York, N. Y.

751.2
C 39e
62673
Sept. 1968

contents

acknowledgments:

The author is greatly indebted to the following people who contributed so much to the development and completion of this book:

Mr. Russell O. Woody, Jr., artist and author, who rendered advice and encouragement, as well as other kindnesses.

Mrs. Beatrice Thompson, art instructor at the John Marshall High School, Los Angeles, who contributed examples of her students' work.

Mr. Harold Stevens, author and art instructor at the Garden School, New York City, who made beautiful photographs for this book.

Mr. Warren Nelson, commercial photographer, whose advice and information on technical matters were most useful.

Mrs. Constance H. Gills, Secretary of the Audio-Visual Aids Department, Longwood College, Farmville, Virginia, who assisted in photographing many of the classroom scenes reproduced.

Particular appreciation is given to the many students who willingly cooperated in portraying phases under discussion in this book. Cited especially for their help are Connie Lou Gills, Patricia Morton, Elizabeth Smith, Barbara Davis, Terry and Anne Hilman, Deanna Talley, Linda Dyer, Mary Arendahl, Elizabeth Broaddus, Celia Carter, Karen Mitchell, Kathryn Reid, Katherine Jarrett, Lea Sowder, Harriet Anderson, and Gloria Logan; also, David Reid, Robert Bruce, Randolph Harper, Mark Hileman, Charles Simonini, Charles Griffin, Larry Prasse, and James Scott.

For centuries artists have sought the perfect painting medium, one which would combine the luminosity, durability, depth, and versatility of oil with the fluidity and immediacy of expression inherent in watercolor. Art teachers have dreamed of an all-purpose medium that would not hinder expression but stimulate it, a relatively inexpensive material, not fraught with technical limitations, that could be used on all classroom levels.

In answer to these needs the last decade has seen the development of remarkable new synthetic media which allow the beginner and professional artist as well as the craftsman and the commercial artist a means of technical accomplishment hitherto impossible with traditional media.

The new synthetic paints have a "built-in" durability and an ease of application that is hard to imagine. They are now used by at least one third of all practicing artists, including such famous contemporaries as James Brooks, Thomas Hart·Benton, Adolph Gottlieb, David Siqueiros, Milton Resnick, Frederic Taubes, Al Held, Glen Alps, and Robert Weaver. A list of names could fill pages, and the number is increasing daily as new brands and formulations proliferate and as new, unique techniques are being discovered.

Synthetic media promise to revolutionize art experiences in the classroom. One material can now be used for all painting techniques from watercolor to oil as well as for sculpture and bas relief, silk screen blockouts, inks, and printing plates. Innumerable craft projects utilize the new media. Seeming to accomplish the impossible, these materials are basically water-suspended plastics or, in some cases, plastic solutions. They are known as *Polymers*.

In addition to the already known advantages of using the Polymer media, unique occurrences and explorational possibilities are always within easy reach of the adventurous artist, teacher, or student. This book will deal with general areas within which the Polymer media are either equivalent to traditional media or superior to them. The teacher and student, to whom this book is directed, are well advised to encourage experimentation toward which these new media lead so willingly. Thus, a free-flowing creative process, coupled with the excitement which Polymers arouse, will provide the kind of kinetic classroom atmosphere desired by every good teacher.

color section

This visually complex, intricately patterned still life was painted from a classroom set-up.
All the main patterns and shapes were painted with unthinned, opaque polymer colors. When these
were dry, glazes of color thinned with the emulsion medium were brushed over the surface
to produce an amazingly rich, glowing effect.

The 14 paintings in the color section
were made by high school students
using Liquitex polymer paint and media.

A figure study painted from life on a gesso ground applied to a heavy cardboard support. (The same ground and support were used for the portraits on the opposite page.) The picture was painted in a scheme of complementary colors using polymer paint opaque and unthinned. Then, brilliant washes and glazes of polymer paint thinned with water and the emulsion medium were applied.

These four portraits, painted from the same student model, were first blocked in with opaque polymer paint. Glazes were added for color and texture.

Polymer paint thinned with water and the emulsion medium was used in a watercolor technique on heavy watercolor paper. The portrait was painted from a student model.

This still life was painted on a gesso ground applied to a chipboard support. The surface was built up thickly with polymer paint. Some areas are painted in very heavy impasto for a strong textural effect.

A marine subject painted on a gesso ground applied to chipboard. Glazes were applied over polymer washes thinned with water and emulsion medium. Finishing details were applied with dry brush technique.

Wooden blocks of various sizes and shapes were applied to a plywood support with white emulsion glue. They were painted with polymer paint, unthinned and thinned with water and emulsion medium, and later glazed for added color richness.

A collage composed of letter and design elements cut from printed matter and transparent colored tissues. The papers were adhered to a heavy cardboard support with the polymer emulsion medium. When the collage was finished, a coat of the medium was applied over the entire surface as a protective covering—and also to prevent the fugitive colors of the tissues from running and fading.

A figure study in polymer paint on a gesso ground applied to a heavy cardboard support. Modeling paste was used to build up a highly textured, low relief surface.

Polymer paint is used opaquely to build up a rich textured surface like that of an oil painting.

Polymer paint is used heavily in some areas in an impasto technique. To create surface contrast, glazes are applied, one over the other, for subtle color effects.

introduction

TRADITIONAL MEDIA

Since his early beginnings man has relied on some kind of pigment and binder to create art. Over the centuries, experimentation has led from animal fats and plant dyes to the more reliable media familiar today. While some media have undergone steady improvement, others, because of a lack of need, high costs, impracticability or better methods, have been eliminated.

Among the media still maintaining a position of respect in the art world are oil, watercolor, tempera, and casein. Encaustic, or painting with wax, has been reassessed as a medium by a few modern artists, while the other four are actively used. Each has its own advantages.

Oil

Oil paint is the most flexible and versatile of all traditional media. It is composed of pigment, filler for stability and viscosity, and a vehicle, usually linseed oil. The intensity of color runs the entire range from muted to very strong. Oil is easy to use but dries slowly. The colors may be thinned for glazes. It is still the preferred medium for those who are not yet using Polymer Emulsion media.

Watercolor

Watercolor is the quickest to execute of the traditional media. It comes in both cake and tube form and dries quickly. Characteristically transparent, it can be made opaque with the addition of white gouache. It may be used as a thin undercoat for other media. Good white paper stock is required, not just for the luminosity it affords, but because water is frequently used to saturate the paper before beginning to work, which will weaken a poor quality paper.

Tempera

Today's poster paint, or commercial tempera, is a fairly reliable opaque paint. It differs from its fine art counterpart, egg tempera, which is formulated with

17

an animal binder rather than a vegetable one. Used exclusively before the middle of the fifteenth century by Western artists, egg tempera has a fine reputation for durability. Whole egg is used for the balance of fatty and lean oils innately combined in nature. Egg tempera was often used as underpainting for oils in the Renaissance.

Casein

Made of curd milk and fat binders, casein has been used for years by artists who desire a medium with reliable adhesion. When used properly, never over 1/16 inch thick and with a prepared milk emulsion and added ingredients, casein affords the student any effect he desires from watercolor to oil.

Encaustic

Encaustic, or painting with wax, an ancient technique, is used by some artists today who apparently enjoy the rich, though matte, colors it makes possible. Employed by the Egyptians and Greeks for surface decoration and in murals, encaustic entails the use of wax made solvent by turpentine and mixed with pigment for application to a support. A heating device, usually a flatiron, is held close to the painted surface in order to fuse the ingredients and draw the wax to the top as a protective shield. Although only minor examples are preserved from ancient cultures, the reliability of the medium is unquestioned.

Fresco

Fresco is a mural technique especially popular during the Renaissance. In the true fresco technique, colors ground in lime water are applied to moist plaster, a small area at a time to prevent the surface from drying out before a section can be finished. A full-size cartoon of the projected work is prepared in advance to insure accuracy in delineation. The technique lends itself to flat wall decoration. Today, the more dependable synthetic media are used for true fresco technique as well as for fresco secco (painting on dry plaster), which is less laborious and intensely colorful.

POLYMER EMULSION MEDIA

Technically speaking, the Polymer Emulsion media, the only synthetic media among the several produced with which we will be concerned, are suspensions of non-toxic, plastic resin particles in water. Evaporation of the water leaves the solid particles bonded into an elastic, yet tough, film which is extremely durable.

In addition to their own characteristics, which permit an amazing range of exploration and surface effect, the Polymer Emulsion media can successfully duplicate the qualities specific to each of the traditional media already discussed. Other advantages of the synthetic Polymer Emulsion colors and media include:
1. High resistance to ultra-violet light or sunlight.
2. Great intensity of color. Unlike watercolor and tempera, Polymer colors retain their initial value as they dry.
3. Complete transparency and opacity may be achieved simultaneously.
4. Unparalleled adhesiveness to almost any non-oily support, from heavy paper to Masonite.
5. Unusual versatility, including sculpture, print making, bas relief, and virtually all painting techniques.
6. No pre-sizing or varnishing necessary.
7. Assured permanence under normal conditions.
8. Compatibility with other media, except those which are not water soluble.

The few disadvantages are more of an integral nature rather than established characteristics. A slight stickiness will occur when paintings are stored in extremely hot areas. This may be avoided or minimized, however, by stacking paintings face-to-back or by placing wax paper between them.

Do not paint on oily, greasy or hard, shiny surfaces such as gloss oils, formica, glass, metals, and waxed wood because the Polymer media will come loose from these surfaces if water is applied. Hardboards, other than Masonite, should be sanded to remove the shine, thus assuring better adhesion.

The Polymers used should be of *one brand name.* None of the Polymer media, which are aqueous, may be mixed directly with oil colors; however, a thoroughly dry oil painting *which has no gloss* may be covered with the Polymer media, and Polymer is an excellent underpainting for oils.

SUPPORTS (Painting Surfaces)

Stiff supports such as untempered Masonite or plywood, properly sized, or fibrous supports such as canvas are essential in order that an oil painting will endure the destructive effects of time. In contrast, the Polymer Emulsion media may be used on virtually any non-oily support from heavy paper to Masonite. Sizing is not required, nor is a ground necessary. The Polymer Emulsion Medium simultaneously establishes protection for both the pigment and the support. Paper or fibrous supports which absorb moisture should be thoroughly pre-coated with Polymer Emulsion Medium.

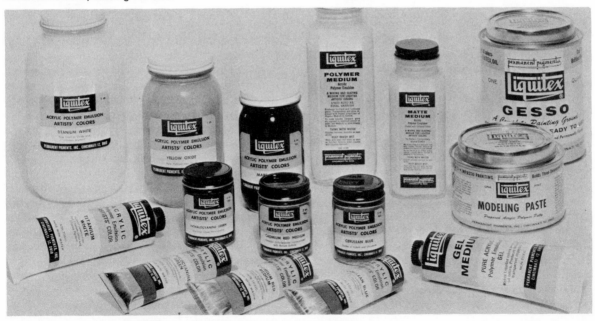

The Acrylic Polymer paints and the various media. The paints are available in jars of various sizes as well as tubes. The media include: Polymer (gloss) Medium, Matte Medium, Gesso, Modeling Paste, Gel Medium, and Matte Varnish.

PAINTING MEDIA

The Polymer Emulsion media include tube and jar water-thinned colors, Polymer vehicles such as Gloss and Matte Medium, Gel Medium, Modeling Paste, Gesso and Polymer Matte Varnish.

Polymer Emulsion Medium, either **Matte** or **Gloss,** is the all-purpose Polymer vehicle. The colors are ground in it, thinned with it, glazed with it, and it can also be used as a final varnish. Matte Medium should not be used as a final coat, however, as it may leave a chalky glaze over dark colors.

Polymer Gel, a salve-like, thickened Polymer Medium, looks milky when applied but dries very clear. Excellent for adding viscosity to a painting mixture, it dries slower than the liquid Medium and is, perhaps, the finest glaze vehicle on the market. Adhering additive materials to a painting support is best done with the Gel Medium.

Matte Varnish, which is used as a protective coating for paintings, can double as a fixative for charcoal or pastel drawings if half diluted with water and sprayed on with an atomizer. When applying it as a varnish, use long, clean strokes with a wide, soft-haired brush.

Polymer Modeling Paste may be used advantageously as a filler to produce impasto paint compounds and greater paint viscosity. It has been used most extensively as a textural device to build raised areas on painting supports or frames as well as relief forms for carving. Modeling Paste may be applied to a papier-mâché form for details and will provide a surface on which to carve a design for relief printing.

Polymer Gesso is the most popular ground coating on the market today. It is strong and pliable as are all the Polymer products. Extremely white, one coat used full strength is sufficient ground for a canvas. If it is used on stiff supports, however, several thin coats are better. Its adhesiveness makes it ideal for incorporating additives.

Heavy duty glass palettes are best for the Polymer Emulsion media. Dried paints or emulsions may be loosened and removed easily by simply brushing the glass with water or soaking stubborn areas. The paints can be easily scraped off the glass and even applied later for surface texture. Other palettes could include formica slabs, oiled boards, porcelain trays, or any hard, shiny surfaces at hand.

PAINTING TECHNIQUES

The great variety of painting techniques made possible by the Polymer Emulsion media are discussed in detail in the following chapters, with special emphasis on the opaque and transparent techniques of oil and watercolor.

Casein techniques are easily executed with the Polymer Emulsion media. By allowing a percentage of water to evaporate from the jar emulsion color, a thickening develops which permits it to be worked similarily to casein. If this mixture lacks the desired body, Modeling Paste, inert clay, or calcium carbonate (whiting) may be added, one part additive to four parts Polymer Emulsion color. Traditional casein used in heavy impasto may develop cracks and peel off the support in time. Polymer Emulsion Medium may be compatibly incorporated with the traditional medium with no yellowing or peeling. The use of Polymer Emulsion Matte Medium will ensure the casein appearance of a painting, and a coating of Polymer Matte Varnish will act as a solid, protective film. Secondary students should be particularly pleased with this technique.

Watercolor may be done in a like fashion with the Polymer Emulsion media. Runny color will be at a minimum on a surface generously coated with the Polymer Emulsion Medium. The color applied directly into the Medium does not run or dissipate in intensity.

Re-wetting the paper with a thick Polymer-water solution will maintain the moist surface. Several factors become important in this connection:

1. The Medium stabilizes the support and prevents paper roll-up to a great extent.
2. Color is held in place by the Medium but may be manipulated in the traditional manner.
3. A clear, transparent film acts as a varnish, sealing in the color without destroying the watercolor effect.
4. When dry, it may be painted over without muddying or picking up the underlying color.
5. If changes must be made, white Polymer Emulsion paint or Polymer Gesso may be brushed over the area and the design begun again.

The entire watercolor painting may be further protected by painting the back with the Medium to encase the whole in a waterproof film.

Unless one is knowledgeable in the art of fresco, he had better not attempt this difficult procedure in the traditional methods. If the wall support is strong, however, anyone may produce the equivalent of a traditional fresco by painting directly on a freshly cleaned wall which is first sized with Polymer Emulsion Medium.

Succeeding applications fuse with the initial coat for a solid bond. The color may be as intense or muted as one desires. The Polymer Emulsion Medium is also a reliable deterrent against the destructive effects of the atmosphere. The decorated walls and panels for murals are attractively done in many schools by the students. The dependability of the Polymer Emulsion media greatly facilitates these projects. In a mosaic wall decoration, blocks of wood, metal, or ceramic tile may be combined and decorated with Polymer Emulsion paints to provide a wider color range than is possible with conventional processes.

Papier mâché, carving, jewelry making, puppetry, and ceramics are areas in which one may work with the Polymer Emulsion media. This versatility means a great deal to the teacher who is concerned about creative opportunities for his pupils.

PRECAUTIONARY MEASURES

All art media impose some problems which must be considered, especially when students are involved. The adhesiveness of the Polymer Emulsion media is such that students should be directed to wear aprons, smocks or some other protective covering when working. Cans of water should be kept readily available for soaking the brushes when they are not actually in use.

Colors to be used at one session might be kept in small plastic ice-cube trays and covered with Saran wrap. Keep the jar tops and tube caps clean and tightly closed on all containers. If a skim should form, any remaining paint underneath it is still usable.

SPECIAL ABILITIES

No special abilities are needed for students to manipulate the Polymer Emulsion media. Whether first grader or senior in high school, the Polymer Emulsion media enable the student to work as he naturally would with the traditional media. As an economy measure, the jar paint may be diluted with 4 to 6 parts water to one of pigment. Add a small amount of Gel Medium or Emulsion for retention of bonding strength. If economy is a great factor, the teacher could profit by using Emulsion alone, as it is an ideal vehicle for paint pigments. When combined with powder tempera it will darken middle tone hues slightly, but it will provide a richer blend than is seen with many powder temperas. Powder pigments mixed with Polymer Emulsion should be used soon after they are mixed, as they often go bad if stored for very long.

part 1

Polymer Media Used in Painting

chapter 1/opaque painting

The term "opaque" refers to a surface through which light cannot pass. In painting, more use is made of opaque coating than any other. Due to the great flexibility of the Polymer Emulsion paints and media, each technical manipulation must be explained separately. Paintings are executed in the traditional opaque manner with any adjustments to be made explained in the following sections treating with each particular technique or medium.

AS OIL PAINT

Polymer Emulsion media achieve an "oil" quality with as much facility as the actual oil medium. This can be accomplished directly with tubed Polymers.

The Gel Medium. A salve-like, viscous painting medium called Gel is also available, which makes an excellent painting medium comparable to the sun-thickened oil resins used in oil painting. It thins with water, mixes easily with the Polymer colors, and enables one to build an opaque painting surface to much greater projective importance than is the case with oil, yet it dries more rapidly than oil paint vehicles. Unlike oils, the Gel impasto layer is not simply congealed, but thoroughly dry in 24 hours.

When the Gel Medium is mixed with the Polymer Emulsion paints, it produces a creamy, viscous opaque mixture which may be applied thickly with either a brush or a palette knife. A ratio of one part Gel to two parts paint is desirable for impasto painting with brush or palette knife. If too much Gel is added, the colors become transparent.

Modeling Paste. Modeling Paste, another Polymer Emulsion accessory item, consisting of pulverized marble dust and Polymer Emulsion, is made whiter by the addition of titanium. The setting time of this excellent impasto medium ranges from two hours to overnight, depending upon the depth of application. Modeling Paste should be applied in multiple layers of no more than 1/16 inch to prevent shrinkage cracks. If Gel is added by one-third to one-half volume to the Paste, high impasto can be accomplished without cracking.

Tools. Any type of brush may be used with the Polymers. Most classrooms are stocked with the well-known black, horsehair bristle brushes and pointed watercolor brushes. Camel hair or hog bristle brushes one to three inches wide, for covering large areas, should also be stocked. Nylon bushes are excellent and less expensive.

For applying the thicker mixtures, table knives, putty knives, small trowels and palette knives may be used. Tongue depressors, plastic squeeze bottles, popsicle sticks or cardboard strips may be employed for applying thick paint. Block print brayers also may be used for this.

Heavy panes of glass about 8 x 10 inches which have been made safe for use by applying masking tape along the edges are excellent palettes for older students. Small baby food jars and plastic ice trays are good paint containers for children. It is well to remember that in easel painting a creamy consistency of color will not run as profusely as the usual water paint. A little Polymer Emulsion Medium added to the color will greatly retard the running of paint.

Sizing and supports. Absorbency in a painting support, which can ruin the surface effects desired, is avoided very simply by applying Polymer Gesso to the surface before starting to work. Its elasticity and strength, as well as its luminosity, leave little to be desired in a ground covering. Illustrators have learned to utilize the accidental textures that occur in applying Gesso. Discerning students may also discover the importance of subtle surface occurrences which are a factor in opaque painting. Decorative paper and other additives may be placed into a wet coating of the Gesso and then re-coated with more of the ground coat to become safely and permanently encased. Surface embellishment is discussed in a later chapter (See Part II, Chapter 7).

Classroom considerations. Experimentation is important to students as an outlet for their natural curiosity. The Polymer Emulsion media will contribute much to a healthy and creative classroom environment.

Secondary students will find Polymer Emulsion colors ideal for illustration and lettering in their commercial art classes. Book jackets, bulletin board displays, Christmas decorations, all can be made richer in color and depth by applying the colors opaquely.

The art teacher will appreciate the rapid drying time of the Polymer colors when applied in a normal thickness, for between classes the paintings may be safely stored away.

Precautions. Disposable palettes such as aluminum foil or wax paper may be used as an aid to cleanliness. During the process of using the Polymer media, students should have a generous supply of water at their disposal. Brushes must be kept in water when not in use, as the media set rapidly and may damage the brushes if they are not kept moist. Glass palettes may be scraped clean with a palette knife or a scraper fitted with a razor blade.

To avoid any damage from the adhesion of two works in the Polymer media, inflexible panels should be stored face-to-back or wax paper should be placed over heavily painted surfaces.

AS TEMPERA

Tempera is best used in a flat, non-transparent manner. The range of the Polymer Emulsion colors greatly exceeds that of the traditional tempera colors. Permanence, a constant consideration for good craftsmanship, is best assured under all conditions with the Polymer media. The advantages of the Polymer Emulsion paints over tempera are:
1. Greater color range, intensity, and permanence
2. Complete color retention when diluted
3. Equivalent or shorter drying time
4. Safer to use on most supports
5. Contain dispersion agents to deter settling
6. Reliably used in combination with other water media
7. Flexible supports may be used and rolled for easy storage.

MIXED MEDIA

The use of Polymer Emulsion enables one to employ more than one method in arriving at an end product. By this is meant that other, more conventional painting techniques may be used with the Polymer Emulsions to achieve a desired result. Dry pigments or prepared dry tempera may be incorporated with the Polymer Medium. A slight discoloration or darkening of tone may be seen with some of the colors. It is advisable initially, in the case of prepared powdered tempera, to mix water with the color until a creamy consistency results. Then the pure, undiluted Emulsion Medium is added to form an adequate painting vehicle. Do not store mixtures of this sort for over one week's time, as some of the dry pigments might go bad. A few pigments react with Polymers immediately and are useless. It is better practice to mix Polymer Medium with tempera colors as one paints, to avoid trouble.

AS CASEIN

Casein is a thicker opaque medium than most temperas. This medium, which is made of curd of milk and is highly adhesive, may be emulated with the Polymer media. Evaporation of some of the water used to mix the Polymer media will bring about a thicker medium which will resemble casein.

SUMMARY

Most painting media are primarily opaque in normal use. The use of the Polymer media offers not only opacity but a large color range as well.

The vehicles of Polymer Emulsion and Gel insure permanence as well as the needed consistency for application. The Gel enables one to produce an impasto surface of great richness equivalent to that done in oil, as well as being able to apply a fine transparent glaze. (See Part I, Chapter 3.)

Because of the elasticity of the Polymer media, painting supports may include anything from a good white vellum to untempered Masonite. Interesting new surfaces are employed and the support need not be sized. This in itself offers great economy to the classroom instructor.

For durability and permanence, applications of the Emulsion Medium are recommended for both sides of a support, as well as the edges.

Precautions are necessary with any plastic medium, and Polymer Emulsion, because of its fine adhesive quality, is no exception. The following are recommended safeguards, both for users and equipment:
1. Brushes should be kept in water when not in use.
2. Aluminum foil may serve as a temporary cover for a paint container, but when stored, jars and tubes must be tightly closed.
3. Hard, shiny or oily surfaces such as glass, formica, metals, oiled boards, etc., are recommended as palettes. (Soaking the palette in water will remove dried plastic paint.)
4. Smocks, aprons or some other protective covering should be used.
5. Though the Polymer media dry rapidly, panels should be stored face-to-back.

Color intensity is retained though color is diluted —an economy asset when Polymer colors are used in the lower grades. Running is minimized by the addition of Polymer Emulsion Medium to the colors. Any brushes are suitable.

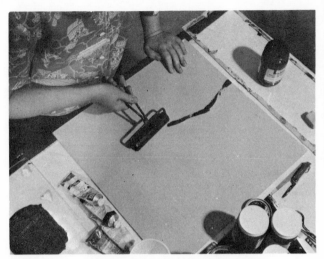

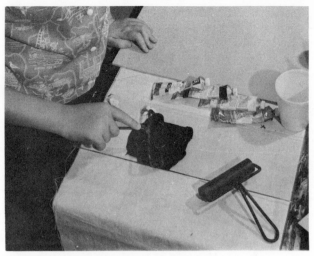

1. The brayer is a good tool to begin the painting. For an opaque effect, the paint is used—without Medium or water as thinners—direct from the tube. A sheet of glass makes an excellent palette.

2. The paint-covered brayer is pressed—without rolling—against the cardboard support to create bold lines.

Making an Opaque Painting with a Variety of Tools

4. Now the brayer is rolled to create the broad mass of the sky.

3. The textural effect of leaves is produced by printing with a sponge dipped in paint.

5. Since Acrylic Polymer paints dry rapidly, layer upon layer can be added quickly without fear of unwanted running or graying of colors.

6. A piece of corrugated cardboard is painted and pressed onto the picture to make a fence.

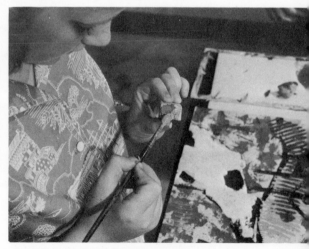

8. Final details are printed on the landscape with a painted art gum eraser.

7. The painted edge of cardboard is pressed into the picture for tree trunks.

The addition of Modeling
Paste or spackle makes
the paint more opaque and
easier to manipulate
for building heavy texture
and relief surfaces.

Virtually any non-oily surface
may be used with Acrylic
Polymer paints. Here a young
artist uses ordinary
classroom paper and easel.

Acrylic Polymer paint applied with a brush
directly from jars as an opaque medium.

29

High school student. Polymer painting on tagboard. A heavy opaque surface is built up with layers of unthinned paint used directly from tubes. After the painting had dried, glazes were added to enrich surface color and texture.

High school student. Heavy opaque layers of paint develop a dry, lumpy effect. The patterned background was glazed over with a transparent color wash.

High school student. Thick layers of Acrylic Polymer paint were applied over a relief surface built up with Modeling Paste to create a heavy, impasto effect.

High school student. Gel Medium and Polymer Modeling Paste were mixed with the Polymer paint to produce a richly textured, low relief surface.

High school student. Rich use of undiluted paint creates a heavily textured, opaque surface.

High school student. Opaque use of Acrylic Polymer paint on a chipboard support with a Gesso ground.

High school student. Acrylic Polymer paint fortified with Gel Medium allowed the student to build up a surface of varied texture.

A surface in the artistic sense is either opaque, translucent, or transparent. Transparent refers to a surface which can be seen through. Window designs, movies, slides, stage-set sections, ceramic glazes, and watercolor techniques all utilize the quality of transparency in various degrees.

WATERCOLOR

Watercolor is characteristically spontaneous, bright, clear in color, and not overworked. Certain procedures are followed to achieve the uniqueness which this popular medium offers. They include preplanning to allow white areas of the paper to be left unpainted, and rendering the large masses of light colors first and the dark colors later. The addition of white paint causes watercolor to become opaque; this is generally avoided. The technique of glazing is employed frequently in watercolor. Succeeding darker colors may be built one over the other until deep, rich tones evolve or more complete definition of form is achieved. Excessive glazing of colors, one over another, however, will produce muddy tones. These techniques require a great deal of skill and practice.

There are, perhaps, more clichés about the use of watercolor than about any other technique. The Polymer Emulsion Medium, however, has done much to broaden the scope of watercolor painting, and to permit certain of the old rules to be put aside.

Comparison of Traditional Watercolor Paints with Polymer Emulsion Paints

WATERCOLOR PAINTS	POLYMER EMULSION PAINTS
1. stock undulates when wet	1. stock flattens when dried
2. easily soiled	2. easily wiped clean
3. must be framed under glass	3. needs no glass protection
4. needs mat in framing	4. medium is self-stiffening
5. colors fade	5. colors never dim
6. requires good paper stock	6. any paper may be used
7. colors muddy in glazing	7. colors remain transparent through glazes
8. highlights must be left unpainted	8. overall color brilliance permits the addition of white highlights

Advantages of the Polymer Emulsion Paints

The Polymer Emulsion paint techniques are the same as those employed for traditional watercolor. They will be applied in the same manner with essentially the same tools, except for the use of Emulsion Medium (either Gloss or Matte). However, a unique depth of watercolor surface is possible.

Whether Polymer Emulsion is used on a dry surface or a pre-moistened one, it becomes an automatic fixing agent—the colors cannot be redissolved when dry. The paint is so adhesive that it will adhere to the support whether or not the paints are thinned with Emulsion Medium. Of significance is the fact that painting onto a surface saturated with Emulsion Medium prevents several things from occurring which have long plagued the watercolorist: The colors do not bleed into one another, colors retain their initial intensity, and mistakes may easily be painted out and redone without harm to the support or the final painting.

This type of repainting may not be done with the traditional medium. When gouache or white is added to watercolor for corrections the quality of transparent watercolor is lost. With the application of Emulsion Medium to moisten the support, white may be freely used, and colors may be applied directly into the white. The resulting muted colors upon drying are covered with an application of Polymer Emulsion Medium. The Polymer Emulsion also assures the painter of a thin dispersion of color so that undesired opaqueness is avoided. Drying is delayed if the surface is sprayed with water from an atomizer.

The usual wrinkling from excessive moisture will not be experienced to any great extent with Polymer Emulsion paints applied to a wet surface. The Polymer film actually stabilizes the support on drying, leveling it and holding it to a desired flatness. It is advisable to coat the back of the watercolor support prior to painting, although this is not necessary. The Polymer Emulsion Medium generally saturates the porous support enough to protect it, but a final coat of Polymer Matte Varnish may be applied as a further protection.

Procedure

A typical procedure for producing a watercolor painting with Polymer Emulsion paints is given in the following steps:

1. Tack the paper support at each corner to a drawing board or attach it with masking tape around all four sides. Stiff cardboard or Upsom board could be used without a heavy drawing board.
2. Pre-moisten the paper thoroughly with water, using a household sponge or a brush.
3. Put a chosen color on a palette and mix it to the desired consistency, adding some Emulsion. A brush too heavily laden with water will cause pigment separation. A drop or two of Emulsion will correct this.
4. Apply color to an area which is to be eventually covered with darker tones; a sky area is a good starting place. This might be followed by a large ground area. White areas may be left unpainted as with traditional watercolor, but since Emulsion is being used, opaque white may easily be brushed into the Emulsion later.
5. Progressively, apply darker, more opaque color into the Emulsion. The Emulsion will fuse with and actually encase the color, keeping it from spreading. If the Emulsion seems to be drying too rapidly, simply apply some water spray. If the Emulsion has set, allow the initial coat to dry, then apply more Emulsion to the support and continue painting.
6. A protective coat of Matte Varnish is recommended for the surface as well as the back of the painting. Matte Medium may be used if the colors are not too dark.

7. If the watercolor paper buckles, wait until the painting is dry, wet the front and back of the paper with a saturated sponge and place the painting under a sheet of Masonite slightly larger than the painting. Weight the Masonite with books if necessary. Within two days the painting will be dry and completely flat. The protective varnish (step 6) will prevent the color from lifting.

Making a Transparent Painting

1. The student begins an undersea painting. To achieve the transparency of a watercolor, Acrylic Polymer paint can be thinned with water or the Emulsion Medium.

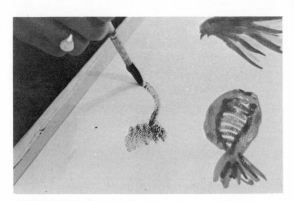

5. Details painted on the moistened paper "bleed" to produce the diffused edges and nebulous effects of true watercolor.

2. Dry brush details are added with unthinned paint.

6. Further details are added to the moistened surface. Here the student incorporates a "mistake" into the composition by making it the eye of a fish.

3. More transparent elements are blocked in with thinned paint.

4. The paper is moistened with a sponge dipped in water.

7. The finished painting reveals a variety of watercolor techniques, including sharp edges, diffused edges, dry brush, and transparent washes.

KITE DECORATION

The most beautiful kites are made with colored tissue. It is possible, however, to use white, translucent tissue for the body of a kite, which can be decorated with transparent Polymer Emulsion colors.

The design should relate to the form of the kite, and for this reason geometric configurations are recommended. Colored tissue combined with the transparent Polymer colors will make a kite of very handsome appearance.

STAINED GLASS PANELS

Stained glass panels provide an intriguing creative experience for young people. One method is to cast plastic shapes with the Polymer Emulsion Medium, as follows:

Once the design has been decided upon, a full-scale mock-up of the design is made. This is taped to a large, flat, horizontal surface. Sheets of polyethylene are taped over it. Then oil-base clay, rolled into thin coils, is applied to the plastic sheeting to define the desired shapes. Next, colored tissue is cut to correspond to the various shapes. Polymer Emulsion Medium is poured carefully into each clay enclosure to a depth of about 1/16 inch. The colored tissue shapes are then laid onto the wet Emulsion. Over the tissue shapes more Polymer Emulsion Medium is poured, until it reaches the height of the clay enclosures. If tissue isn't available, colored cellophane is recommended. It is also possible to laminate crayon colors between two sheets of wax paper with a warm iron. This then is encased exactly as the tissue would be.

The plastic shapes being cast require from one day to two days to set firmly. Then the clay is carefully removed, and Polymer Emulsion black color is either poured or extruded by plastic squeeze bottle or tubes into the spaces left by the removed clay.

The bonding characteristic of Polymer Emulsion causes all separate layers of plastic to become as one. The cast design, however, needs reinforcement. If possible, two sheets of Plexiglas could be attached to enclose the entire panel of cast shapes. Glass mounted into a wooden frame could be similarly used. The panel can be hung near a window to utilize the play of light in the manner of true stained glass.

POLYMER MEDIUM AND CHALK

Another interesting experience in transparency that may be enjoyed by younger pupils involves using colored chalk. The best procedure for this technique is to draw directly into a wet Polymer Emulsion coating. (Drawing on a dry surface to be covered later with Polymer Emulsion Medium is also feasible.) If the Emulsion is kept thin and is applied thinly, the results will be better. The chalk drawing is made in the usual manner; it may be spread by smudging once it is laid into the coating of Emulsion. Broad-stroke drawing with the side of the chalk may be done. When this is dry, the entire surface is re-coated with thinned Matte Varnish. Upon drying, the chalk drawing is encased in layers of Polymer Emulsion Medium. It will not smudge.

Interesting results occur when chalk is used in combination with various other materials. Colored tissue, for example, could be applied to define the major masses; ink could be used for details, while chalk might be employed for pattern and texture. It is possible, too, to cover ink or chalk with tissue layers before adding the final Emulsion coat.

Applying a coat of Polymer Emulsion.

Drawing with chalk directly into the wet Polymer Emulsion coating.

the film is easily scraped clean with a razor blade or pen knife after it has been loosened with a solvent such as 3% hydrogen peroxide. Of course, old, exposed film which is solid black or film liners which are translucent and cream colored are most desirable if you do not have absolutely clear film.

Polymer Emulsion colors may be used as a coloring agent. The color is applied directly to clear film, or lines may be scraped into blackened film emulsion over which color is then applied. A combination of "positive" and "negative" lines or images is interesting.

One must remember that 16mm film travels through the camera at 24 pictures a second. Thus, one design must be repeated in 24 frames for every second of projection.

FILM MAKING

Experimental film making with art materials can be fun. Most of us are familiar with some of the popular experimental films shown in classrooms, such as Norman McLaren's "Fiddle Dee Dee." These films are actually hand made by applying colored inks directly to motion picture film stock.

Making these films is quite simple. Materials include colored cellophane, tincture of merthiolate, mercurochrome, cellophane tape, India and colored inks, or anything transparent, adhesive, and flexible. Cheap film stock may be bought from manufacturers as rejects, dealers' surplus, or one might first check the audio-visual aids department of his school system for old, obsolete film. The emulsion side of

COLORED INK

Colored ink in bottles may be used with Polymer Emulsion Medium. One will find that in mixing the ink with the Emulsion Medium a depth of color akin to that achieved with watercolor is possible. And more important perhaps is the fact that simultaneously a protective coating becomes an automatic fixing agent for the color.

This combination of ink and Polymer Emulsion Medium may also be seen to stabilize the weight of white vellum; and, it could provide a nice underpainting for repeated glazing layers. Too, underpainting with the modern Polymer Emulsions simplifies the entire process, and the brief drying time involved is a decided advantage.

High school students. These four studies were painted from a student model posing as Flora. Heavy white paper was used as a support. The paintings were begun with transparent washes of Acrylic Polymer paint thinned with water and/or Polymer Emulsion Medium. As the paintings progressed, opaque areas and dry brush details were added to contrast with the transparent surface. As in true watercolor, the white paper was allowed to show through in places to create a feeling of luminosity.

High school student. Still life was built up with thin washes of Acrylic Polymer paint on watercolor paper. Final details were added with pen and ink.

High school student. Flower still life painted on a Masonite panel with a Polymer Gesso ground. Thin washes permit much of the white Gesso ground to show through, which adds vibrancy to the colors. Details were drawn with pen and ink.

High school students. Marine studies painted on chipboard with a Gesso ground. A combination of thick, opaque areas and thin, transparent washes.

High school student. Transparent Polymer washes on watercolor paper.

Glazing is a process of applying transparent color coatings to a surface, which has been used in the production of paintings since the fifteenth century.

While glazing can be used to mute bright colors which appear too garish, it is most often employed to create rich tones in a painting. A glaze may be used either to add a subtle warmth to an area or to subdue it. Glazes, too, offer an interesting way of treating areas to act as buffers between extremes of color range and intensity. Few artists will create works of art which are made of either all pure hues or completely of muted ones.

ADVANTAGES OF THE POLYMER EMULSIONS

The Polymer Emulsion media offer definite advantages in glazing experienced with no other media. The ease and simplicity with which they may be handled, the flexibility inherent in the polymerized plastic film, plus their durability and permanence, make the Polymer media superior to any other. The only disadvantage which may occur is a surface stickiness which could bond undesired objects to it if a glazed support is placed in a hot storage area. This has been an unpleasant feature of both co-polymer and aqueous acrylic media but is less true of the acrylic. With the Matte Medium and the Matte Varnish stickiness is less likely to occur. Otherwise, the flexibility of the tough glaze films provides a contractual allowance which enables them to withstand extreme punishment.

HOW TO APPLY A GLAZE

Before discussing ways in which glazing can be used in student art projects, such as oil and water-color painting as well as collage, a brief survey of professional uses of glazing may open up new possibilities for classroom experimentation. Glazes may be achieved in various ways, and not always by the application of transparent films. Like masters of the past, many modern artists find it difficult to paint on a white, untinted ground.

Tinting Grounds

Artists were trained to rely on building a composition on the basis of a series of dark and light masses on a tinted ground. In the past, the tinted ground, achieved by the use of colored turpentine wash, formed the general, dominant middle tone range of the important areas of the composition. When these areas were established one could move quickly to fill in the values above and below the middle tone tint. Today, many artists who have turned to the Polymer media continue to employ the method described above. Polymer Gesso provides an interesting pattern when glazed with an initial tint on which to paint the important focal masses.

Scumbling or Dry Brush Method

This method of opaque glazing involves lightly dry-brushing a viscous mixture over a textured, or raised, area on a painting.

Rubbing

This process of negative glazing entails the application of a full strength opaque color over another color mass after which the glaze is wiped away by hand or cloth. Just enough Polymer Emulsion is added to the color for adhesive strength and protection. One result of this method is the filling in of low lying textured areas with color. It is in direct opposition to scumbling, though the ultimate effect is the same except that the highermost textured portions are wiped clean of color.

Transparent Films

This technique involves the standard glaze procedure of tinting up or shading down a ground color by the use of one brush application over it. The desirable consistency of color and medium is achieved with the salve-like Gel Emulsion. The strength of the Gel insures excellent adhesion and dries very rapidly when applied thinly.

WHICH MEDIUM IS USED FOR GLAZING

In addition to the Polymer Emulsion colors, either liquid or Gel Emulsion Mediums are recommended. In the case of opaque glazing, little Emulsion Medium is used; with the transparent technique, about three to four parts Polymer Emulsion Medium mixed with one part color should prove an ideal painting mixture.

GLAZING AND OTHER MEDIA
In Emulation of Oil

The tried and proven technique of building pictures primarily with layers of glazes may be used with the Polymer Emulsion media. Polymer offers greater assurance of performance with no chemical after effects which plagued traditional painters, and the rapid drying of the Polymer media shortens the sequence of work periods.

If one enjoys the wet-in-wet approach to painting, the Gel Medium will enable him to experience a unique kind of semi-transparent painting. Liberal portions of the Gel Medium are applied to a support on which equally liberal portions of Emulsion color are applied. The addition of inert additives such as finely pulverized pumice, fine sand, powdered clay, or spackling compound will contribute viscosity as well as some alteration of color intensity. The Gel Medium mixed thoroughly into the additives bonds firmly to the support due to its absorptive powers and creates a semi-matte finish.

With Watercolor

Polymer media glazes may be used with the transparent watercolor technique to make a painting of unusual richness and subtlety. They may be used to complement the initial transparent composition. Opacity of forms in the foreground may contribute to the effect of aerial perspective in which forms become muted as they recede into space.

With Collages

Collages frequently require some relief from the total synthesis. As an additive, transparent colored tissue provides variety. The colors are not fast, but this may be decoratively utilized or, if preferred, minimized considerably by the protective film afforded by the Polymer Emulsion Medium. (See Part II, Chapter 6.)

In painting on paper with Polymer Emulsion Medium, the richness of the color affords the artist effects usually possible only with the more expensive silk screen. Polymer Emulsion colors come in 30 to 35 intense colors, including as many as five variations of one hue.

Transparent washes and an "ink" line are possible using extreme dilution of the Emulsion. Colors mixed with Polymer Emulsion are "fixed" firmly, and one need not worry if water is spilled on the surface after a drawing is dry.

SPECIAL CLASSROOM USES

Stained glass windows, already discussed in Chapter 2 under "Transparent Painting," may become part of any comprehensive art program.

Perhaps the easiest stained glass technique is laminating objects between wax paper sheets. Wax crayon scrapings and chips, thread, colored tissue, even leaves and flowers, may be sealed within two sheets of wax paper, and pressed together with a warm iron. Newspaper over and under the wax paper prevents the melted wax from adhering to the iron. Black Polymer Emulsion could be used as a "leaded" defining line around the shapes.

Polymer Emulsion colors, if thinned to glaze consistency, may be painted on cellophane, then matted and framed. If no iron is available a sheet of cellophane which has been stretched and taped to a window of cardboard may be coated with a layer of Polymer Emulsion Medium. Color tissue shapes could then be glued to this film of plastic over which another coating of Medium is applied. A cardboard window, matching the first one, would then be glued to designs rendered on cellophane by using either a commercial white glue or the Polymer Emulsion. White glues in plastic bottles are a more brittle form of Polymer Emulsion, and are not as reliable as the manufactured emulsion plastic sold for use in artwork.

Older children could frame panes of glass to which objects dipped into Polymer Emulsion Medium could be applied, and the Emulsion will immediately begin to "set." The Polymer Medium is anything but totally defined today and offers the curious student the never-ending opportunity of discovering new things previously unknown to him.

A New York gallery exhibited a form which involved the use of several plates of heavy glass mounted vertically in a wooden base. As one looked through the panes painted with repeated geometric shapes, the transparent colors were optically mixed. Though not true glazing, the principle was the same.

Some artists prefer to apply a colored Emulsion and then wipe it away allowing the stained area to act in a transparent or translucent manner with other colors.

The classroom may be the scene for these and other much simpler experiments with the Polymer Emulsions. Scumbling or dry-brushing, semi-opaque glazing, and transparent glazing are all easily achieved on designs requiring grayed hues which might appear more congruous with the whole. Perception, always a concern in artistic growth, is increased through exploration of how one color affects another. Glazed color may also be used to tint an enclosed mass without affecting the contour line.

Experimentation is the key to discovering how

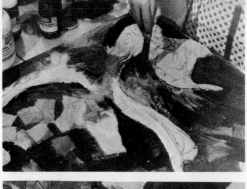

glazes may best function for the artist or student who seeks interesting new ways to use old techniques.

Other methods which could be done in the classroom involve drawing in charcoal or waterproof marking pen on newsprint. A charcoal drawing, which has been spray-fixed, is coated on the reverse side with Polymer Medium or Gel and affixed to a support likewise coated, thus assuring a permanent bond. The drawing is then given a protective coating of Polymer Medium or Gel into which color in dry pigment form or pre-mixed solution is brushed to produce soft, diffused effects. An interesting relationship of two media is seen, as well as a unique handling of line and color.

**Glazing
over
Additives**

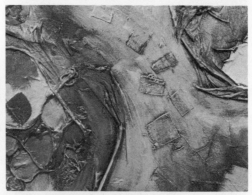

Dipped string, textiles, tissue and pre-cast Polymer forms are incorporated into the adhesive Gesso ground of a Masonite support and glazed with dry brush, transparent washes, and opaque Polymer color.

45

High school student. Beginning with thin washes of Polymer Emulsion Medium, colors above and below the middle tone range are built up to a heavy surface and given a final brilliant glaze of heavier wash.

High school student. A combination of heavy opaque color and washes of transparent Emulsion Medium are applied with a scumbling technique to create an airy sky and watercolor effect adding details sketched in with black dry brush lines.

High school student. Carefully constructed with basic washes on chipboard with a Gesso ground, surface layers are heavily textured using thick tube colors. A final quick glaze of Emulsion Medium is used for surface transparency.

High school students. These paintings with a rough surface texture in heavy impasto of Polymer Modeling Paste applied with the palette knife were dry in a comparatively short time and attractively finished with colored Emulsion Medium washes and dry brush glazes.

High school student. This classic painting on a heavy white paper support primed with Emulsion Medium was done in washes of Acrylic Polymer color and developed with black dry brush lines.

High school student. A strong figure study on gessoed chipboard with washes and heavier Emulsion glazes in alternating layers to achieve a brilliant subtlety of color and line.

High school student. The heavy white paper support for this painting was pre-textured in certain areas with sand adhered into the base coating of wet Emulsion. Successive thin washes of color were augmented with areas of heavy paint, and final glazes over the textured areas unify the composition.

CARL A. RUDISILL LIBRARY
LENOIR RHYNE COLLEGE

Three kinds of additives may be used to create surface texture: linear, fibrous, and granular. Additive materials may be used as textural devices in a painting medium prior to painting or as visual inducements in themselves.

New discoveries in all areas of art media are constantly being perfected. Exploration of new and different ways to use materials is logical and one will discover his own technique which may be entirely suitable.

Additive Materials: white and colored tissue, pelon, tulle, netting, cheesecloth, cotton, burlap, sackcloth, muslin, broadcloth, canvas, aggregates such as Perlite, Celite, Perltex, Xonolite, pumice, spackle, beaded or crushed glass, sand, clay, sawdust, coffee grounds, marble dust, egg shells, string, thread, fiberglas insulation, asbestos, barium sulfate, powdered carborundum, dried plastic skims, and palette scrapings.

Texture additives should always be a supplement. They should be applied in order to enhance a surface in need of variation, or used directly with a painting medium. The Polymer Emulsions encourage the exploration of textural possibilities. Their adhesiveness makes bonding very simple. It is easy to affix a variety of relief materials to a surface before any application of color; or one may use an additive, such as inert clay, to apply texture directly.

Linear additives may be applied directly into a wet medium. String, for example, may be laid directly onto a surface liberally coated with Polymer Gesso, which encases the string, ensuring reliable strength and adhesiveness. However, the string may be dipped into the Gesso before being arranged and then placed slowly where it is needed in the composition. Linear additives may also be pre-affixed before any ground coating is applied.

Additive line may be used to define a mass as one would use a pencil or brush. It can separate areas as well or decorate masses for a design motif. Linear additives can be glued to objects which are themselves then applied as projecting additives.

Experimenting with physical changes in the surface of a painting is now a common technique in art. The flexible softness of tissue and the adhesiveness of Polymer Gesso work together to establish a most interesting pre-painted surface. The procedure is the same as with string in that the tissue is placed into a generous layer of Polymer Gesso. After its initial placement, the tissue may be manipulated to show either flat or wrinkled areas of texture, or it may be pushed into raised linear structures. When the Gesso is dry, another coat is brushed over it. A surface handled in this way provides a most interesting foundation for glazes, drybrushing, or a combination of both. Polymer Emulsion paints deposit enough color into the wrinkled recesses of the tissue to contribute to its added dimension.

Textile additives, not as flexible as tissue, are best applied flat. However, they may be affixed to a support before paint is applied, or within two generous layers of Polymer Gesso.

The fibrous additives vary in textural quality. Burlap is a thick, rough textile of loose weave, while cheesecloth and nylon mesh are quite subtle and much lighter. Many of these may be used in the same composition, although cheesecloth makes a more satisfactory simulated canvas texture.

The entire painting need not be textured. Interesting relationships within the compositional space occur when a dynamic effect between texture and smoothness or projection and recession exists.

Nylon mesh hosiery offers the artist both a pattern and projection and may also be manipulated in any direction.

The easiest additive to apply, granular particles may be mixed with a painting emulsion, sprinkled on wet paint or brushed on with Gesso for a ground. However, remember that most additives of the granular variety should be completely saturated with Polymer Medium to overcome absorptiveness prior to application on a painting support. If the particles are of lightweight materials or are non-absorbent they may be used as they are.

USE OF EXTENDED PROJECTIONS

Unusual materials for painting texturally, such as paper tubes, bottle caps, plastic insulation, and even small boxes, are best used when additives such as thin cloth or facial tissue are saturated with the Polymer Emulsion Medium and pressed securely to the projective additive and to the support which has been coated generously with the Polymer Emulsion Medium. White emulsion glue should be used as a pre-caution when adhering projections such as paper tubes, small boxes, and wooden blocks. For designs using such projections a stiff support is essential.

SGRAFFITO OR INCISED DESIGNS

Prehistoric man relied on carving to express his regard for supernatural spirits or animals, for which he had the greatest respect. Cave walls have revealed configurations which were scratched by Paleolithic man to record his responses to his environment. Jean Dubuffet, today, is famous for his painting surfaces of heavy impasto into which he incises child-like drawings of figures. And who hasn't traced linear portrayals in moist sand?

These techniques, no longer primitive efforts, should appeal to students who profess little drawing ability and may be most content with this tactile and effective method of two-dimensional delineation which is really very simple.

Polymer Modeling Paste is applied on a stiff panel of plywood, Masonite, Celotex, or siding. Modeling Paste may be the commercial Polymer variety, or it could consist of Polymer Emulsion mixed with fine pumice, sand, Perlite, Perltex, glass beads, or marble dust. A spatula, palette knife, putty knife, or tongue depressor may be used to spread the mixture on a panel coated with a clear Polymer Emulsion Medium. When an application of from $\frac{1}{8}$ to $\frac{1}{4}$ inch has been evenly spread on the block, it is allowed to dry overnight. To prevent heavy layers of Modeling Paste from cracking, add ⅓ to ½ Gel Medium. The more Gel Medium added the harder the Paste is to carve. Polymer Emulsion colors may be added to the Paste prior to applying it.

Before the student is ready to execute his ideas, he should do a few preliminary "thumbnail" sketches to plan his work, although Polymer Modeling Paste can be easily patched to remove mistakes. Once the idea is established he may either draw directly onto the block, chalk the back of his sketch identically the size of the block, or he may use carbon paper for transferring his design. He then proceeds to incise a line on the surface of the Modeling Paste with a scriber, compass point, knife, or nail. Patterns may also be scratched within the perimeter of shapes to aid in differentiating one form from another.

These designs may be colored by thin layers of Polymer Emulsion color used as a glaze, by opaque colors painted on the surfaces within the lines or in the incisions by extruding a mixture of color, Polymer Emulsion Medium, and a little Modeling Paste from a squeeze bottle.

Blocks covered with a Modeling Paste mixture may also be carved in a low relief. (See Part II, Chapter 9.)

Painting with a Variety of Additive Materials

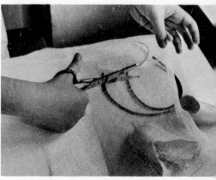

1. A ⅛-inch untempered Masonite support (chipboard will do) is given a coating of Gesso.

2. String and other additives are pressed into the wet Gesso. More Gesso is brushed over the string and additives to affix them to the surface.

3. Cheesecloth makes a subtle textured additive.

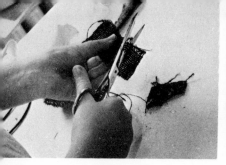

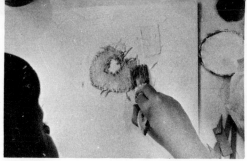

4. Cutting out pieces of burlap—an interesting variety of shapes and patterns.

5. A burlap cut-out is affixed to the painting with Gesso. More than one application may be necessary for good adhesion.

6. Granular additives, such as dried coffee grounds or ground pumice, can be sprinkled onto wet Gesso for increased surface interest.

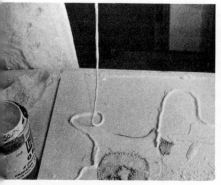

7. String dipped in Gesso is laid onto the Gesso ground to create lines in high relief.

8. Scraps of cardboard or wood can be added with Gesso as a binder.

9. The painting as it appears with all of the additive materials affixed to its surface with Gesso, prior to the application of Acrylic Polymer Emulsion colors.

10. Color can be added to the relief surface with opaque paint or thin transparent glazes.

11. A mixture of Acrylic Polymer paint and Modeling Paste (for added bulk) is extruded from a plastic squeeze bottle to further enrich the surface.

12. Final details are added with a brush.

Cheesecloth is brushed
into a wet Gesso ground
for added texture.

High school student. High relief has been achieved
by adding small wooden blocks to the picture surface with
Emulsion Medium used as glue and varnish.

High school student. On a chipboard support a
highly textured surface was built up with a mixture of Gel
Medium and sand. The student then painted over
this ground with glazes of Acrylic Polymer
paint thinned with Polymer Emulsion Medium.

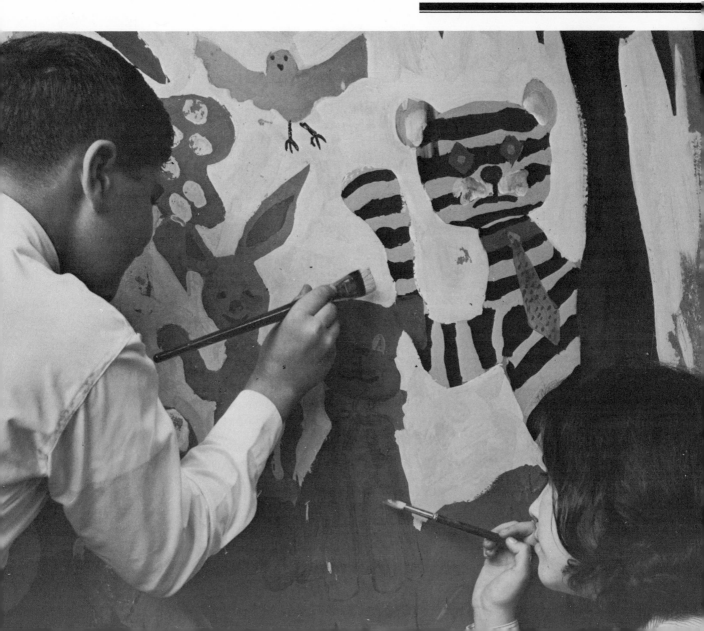

Murals are large wall paintings. Often associated with particular events and famous places, the mural is an idiom which has demonstrated its cultural importance. Most of us are familiar with Michelangelo's Sistine frescoes in Rome, Pompeii's murals, the exterior murals by Rivera and Sequeiros in Mexico, or those seen in many of our public buildings.

We know, too, that murals were not always rendered in oil. Fresco, a popular technique during the Renaissance, was used to produce great works of art, but it is laborious and requires great skill. Artists of Bonampak, a Mayan cultural center of Pre-Columbian Guatemala, produced what have been called by some the most beautiful frescoes of all time. And, of course, we are all familiar with the profile configurations of Egyptian murals. Today, with the Polymer Emulsion media, it is possible to produce murals which have greater permanence, more intensity and variety of color, and which require less effort and time. These advantages and the development of new, improved building materials have revolutionized the art of mural painting—still a favorite way of embellishing interior and exterior wall space.

CONTEMPORARY METHODS

Before discussing techniques designed especially for classroom use, a brief review of contemporary professional approaches to mural painting using the new Polymer media will provide a background for later student experimentation.

There are several ways in which one may prepare a surface for mural painting. Murals are frequently painted in the studio, rolled, and conveyed to the area of exhibition. They are then affixed directly to a wall surface using the dependable acrylic adhesives. No danger exists, however, in contraction and expansion when the acrylics are used. Oil painting may be used to create such a work, but most artists today rely on the Polymer Emulsions, painting on canvas over a reinforced wooden frame or on canvas glued to panels of Masonite, Fiberglas, or Plexiglas. Polymer media may also be applied directly to plaster, concrete, and cinder block.

Perhaps the best support for a mural is a false wall erected in front of an existing one. Expansion and contraction problems, moisture absorption, and peeling of paint are all circumvented in this way. No fibrous covering is required. Untempered Masonite panels have proved most practical for this purpose. They should be hung in a seasoned wood frame glued and cross-braced at the back. A frame within which the Masonite may expand is preferable, as Masonite does expand and contract.

After a frame within which the panel may "ride" is completed, it may then be attached to the inner framework of the plaster wall by toggle bolts or extension bolts. Prior to handling the panels it is advisable to seal the back with acrylic resins or lacquer. If more than one panel is used for the mural, the seams between them must be sealed. One-eighth to one-quarter inch should be allowed between panels over which is glued a muslin or linen band about an inch wide. Contraction-expansion problems are countered in this way. If a ridge is present because of the band, coat the panels with five to six applications of either Polymer Emulsion Gesso or Titanium White Emulsion color.

Several things should be kept in mind when painting a mural. First, complete reliance on the paint thinned *only* with Polymer Emulsion Medium is necessary. The use of water for thinning the paint will weaken the bonding power of the Polymer media. Secondly, due to the conditions under which the mural must exist, one should apply Polymer Matte Varnish or Polymer Gloss Medium to the painting. If the mural is to hang outdoors, protective coatings of acrylic resin (not aqueous Polymer Emulsions) should be applied to the surface.

One professional procedure for painting a mural using more than one panel is as follows:

1. Once the subject has been decided upon, sketches are made. If the design is of a non-representational nature, a series of guide sketches in color is needed.
2. A mock-up is made the identical size of the mural, or a smaller drawing is made to the exact scale of the finished painting. Charcoal, Conté crayon, or graphite stick can be used. Grid lines may be established on the mock-up for an accurate guide in the transferral from sketch to final surface.
3. The panels are coated with from three to six layers of Gesso, which are sanded between applications.
4. The design is transferred to the panel by pouncing chalk through perforations on the drawing, or traced by redrawing over the back of the sketch and using pressure to apply the design to the panel.
5. One of several procedures may follow:
   a. A series of transparent glazes may be applied, over which successive glazes and ultimate opacity will ensue.
   b. The establishment of major dark and light masses in the colors to be used in the final rendering.
   c. A complete underpainting in a monochromatic range of colors either by glazes, opaque masses, or both.
   d. A tinting of the ground coat with a glaze over the sketch which has been more fully established in ink line or dark Polymer Emulsion color.
   e. A complete start-to-finish rendering on each form as it is seen to be focally important; or, painting in opaque colors on the massive "negative" areas around the important forms.
6. The panels are hung after being attached to the frame or support. Before hanging, panels are coated with Polymer Emulsion Medium on all surfaces.
7. The seams are then covered with linen and Polymer Emulsion Medium and touched up with paint to match the surrounding painted areas.
8. The finished work is coated evenly with Polymer Emulsion Matte Varnish or Gloss Medium. Exterior murals necessitate the use of non-aqueous acrylic resins for adequate protection against the elements.

A mural may be made by enclosing spaces on a sheet of glass or formica with oil-base clay into which color mixed with Emulsion Medium is poured, to set. Different shapes and colors composed of bits of colored glass, glass beads, cellophane, buttons, or anything small and transparent are put into the puddles of Emulsion. After two days of drying, the clay rings are removed, the plastic shapes are also easily removed with water and a razor blade, after which they are glued with Polymer Emulsion to a large sheet of glass or Plexiglas. Another sheet of glass of equal size is placed over the previous one and the project is enclosed by a frame. It may then be used as a room divider, pseudo stained glass panel, or illuminated table top, as well as a mural.

One may encase natural forms such as leaves, butterflies, seeds, etc., in Polymer Emulsion alone. However, even when cast as a thick layer, it will be flexible and some reinforcement is needed. Heavy-duty glass panes are recommended to be used on both sides of the cast panel.

One thinks of traditional murals in terms of one plane, but a series of translucent or opaque panels could be juxtaposed. In churches, schools, hallways, and office buildings murals are an excellent solution to the never-ending effort of integrating art and architectural form.

IN THE CLASSROOM

Making murals is a valuable creative experience for young people. Murals may be made with a great variety of media including wax crayons, chalk, ink, tempera, watercolor, and photographs. They may be enhanced by the use of collage components or applied shapes which have been rendered by crayon rubbings, spattering ink or tempera on paper, chalk smudging, watercolor or ink applied to a wet surface, and sponged patterns in tempera. One may stamp print with carved potatoes, erasers, or wooden blocks, or stencil through an opening in a cardboard form. A paint roller may be used for special effects.

Mural activities relate to other learning areas. At one school, four children in correlation with English reading class were to illustrate a poem in a very brief time. Using chalk on colored construction paper, they were told to draw a significant incident. The separate drawings were to be assembled later to form a mural. The result was interesting and the audio-visual collaboration was well received by other children in the class. However, the delightful chalk mural was difficult to save. Plastic sprays should have been used. A sponge dipped into a diluted Polymer Emulsion Medium and wiped on the paper prior to drawing would have preserved its brilliance and avoided smudging.

Polymer Emulsion colors are perfect for classroom projects in mural painting. The process may be adjusted to interest various age groups from elementary to high school level. The brilliance of the colors is retained even when they are diluted four parts water to one part color. The addition of a little transparent Polymer Medium will automatically aid in adhesion to the painting support. All brushes should be kept in water when not being used for painting.

The Polymer Emulsion colors are not only richer than standard tempera colors but are available in more than 30 colors. All Polymer supplies should be purchased in ONE BRAND LINE only, both for economy in bulk prices and to avoid mixing various brands which may have different chemical structures and consequently not work well together.

Once a week the teacher should thoroughly clean the brushes in brush cleaner or lacquer thinner. Due to the toxic and inflammable nature of the solvents, children should not handle them. The weekly dipping of brushes into the solvent will extend the life of the brushes.

1. The teacher discusses the students' preliminary drawing. Ordinary rolled butcher paper is a satisfactory surface for Acrylic Polymer paints. Druggist bond, building paper, and brown Kraft paper may also be used.

2. Painting over the preliminary sketch.

**Mural Painting
as a
Classroom
Project**

3. Blocking in large elements with a bristle brush.

4. Since Acrylic Polymer paints dry rapidly, overpainting can be done almost immediately.

5. Here colors are being applied unthinned from the jar with bristle brushes.

6. Because of its consistency, Acrylic Polymer Emulsion color enables one to do lettering with a fine brush.

7. Combined opaque and transparent effects enliven the surface. The opaque quality of Acrylic Polymer Emulsion colors enables one to apply one color over another without loss of color strength.

8. Painting opaque-on-opaque details with a fine brush. Juxtaposition of Acrylic Polymer Emulsion colors provides a surface of great richness.

9. Before adding larger lettering and connecting the design areas.

10. The group mural nears completion.

High school student. Small mural panel, 4 x 6 feet. Thin washes of Acrylic Polymer paint (diluted with water and the Emulsion Medium) on heavy butcher paper.

DIORAMA

One could call the popular diorama designs "three-dimensional pictures." Young students like to explore ways of creating the illusion of space in their design. Peep boxes done in a shoe box with holes to see through are fun. Mobiles are interesting to make. Stabiles teach a child how to use a variety of materials to create a three-dimensional equilibrium. Dioramas provide an exciting transition from two- to three-dimensional design. Polymer Emulsions provide added realism on which dioramas, like stage sets, depend.

Dioramas are usually made in either of two ways: the suspension of cutout, two-dimensional shapes in the box space, or modeled forms in open space. Depth is the important factor, and frequently walls are inverted to intensify this effect. Elaborate, permanent cyclorama walls can be constructed with the Polymer Emulsions which insure durability and usefulness for future designs in the same space. Such a project was done by artist Allan D. Jones for Mariner's Museum in Newport News, Virginia. It is an immense project measuring 18 feet in width and 6 feet in depth. The backdrop was a Fiberglas shell. The water area was done on Masonite paneling with additive for ripples of water. The river banks were carved from Polymer Modeling Paste; trees and foliage were made by soaking paper in glycerin to maintain softness, and then painting with Polymer Emulsion Medium for stiffening. Pine trees were made of skeleton wire forms covered with drops of Gel Medium and dipped into container of crushed walnut hulls; powdered green pigment was then dusted over the trees.

Tents and buildings were cast in plaster of Paris from modeling clay molds, while the figures were made by dipping plastic fishing line into a mixture of Polymer Emulsion Medium and Modeling Paste and later painted with Polymer Emulsion colors. A variety of additives was used to make a realistic Civil War naval battle scene. Cotton was plastic sprayed to look like smoke, and egg shells, sponge, and thread were incorporated in the scenic spectacle. Great dependence was placed on the durability and drying speed of the Polymer Emulsions.

part 2

Relief and Three Dimensions

Shortly after the turn of the century, the term *papier collé*—literally, "pasted paper"—was adopted by the Cubists in France to describe a composition of papers and other odds and ends. Today, we know the art form as *collage*. The Cubists had discovered that by breaking up masses into a pattern of two-dimensional planes they could better relate form we perceive three-dimensionally to the flatness of a picture surface. This concept, advocated in principle for centuries, was not unique, but the differentiated patterning of individual elements was. From an emulation of real patterns, a Braque innovation, to a more random process of patterning for the sake of design, a Picasso invention, the merit of collage was established. To this day collage holds an important place in two-dimensional artistic expression.

SUPPORTS

Collages, which are actually low-relief constructions, may be built up on any surface. Unless one uses an adhesive which has elasticity, however, the tension of contraction and expansion can be harmful. Bonding can be affected when animal glues are used, as they may crack and cause the collage pieces to fall off. Polymer Emulsion media, on the other hand, will adjust to any movement of the support with no damage to the collage.

The use of a rigid support is recommended. Untempered Masonite is preferred by many artists; its smoothness may be cut by rough sandpaper to develop enough "tooth" for sound adhesion. Upsom board, plywood, and Celotex are other compressed panels which may be used satisfactorily. These pan-

els will absorb moisture readily, however, and should be primed with Polymer Emulsion Medium. The Emulsion Medium, brushed over front, back, and edges, actually encases the entire panel in a tough, moisture-proof and durable plastic film.

ADHESIVES

Few adhesives surpass the Polymer media. They are completely dependable, serving both as adhesive and varnish. Many artists and students rely on the white emulsion glues (such as Elmer's) for adhesives. These are sold in plastic squeeze bottles and are usually Polymer mixtures composed of polyvinyl acetate emulsified with added ingredients and diluted with water to produce a product comparable to the commercial Polymer art media. There is a vast difference between the two types, however; the white glue does not contain the better quality ingredients nor those necessary for dependable durability.

TRANSPARENT COLLAGE

The most popular method of making a transparent collage involves the use of colored tissue and the Polymer Emulsion Medium. Beautiful designs are possible with a simple procedure which features the colorful interplay of two or more colors. Great richness and beauty of contrast is assured when the support has been pre-coated several times with Polymer Gesso. When all component parts have been adhered to the support with the Medium and the collage surface has set and dried, the completed work is given a coating of Polymer Gloss Medium or Matte Varnish.

Using Tissue Papers

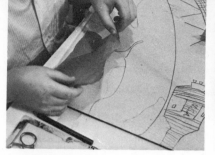

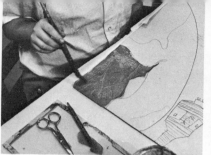

A cut-out piece of tissue paper is lowered in place over a section coated with Polymer Emulsion Medium.

The tissue is brushed firmly into position with a brush loaded with Polymer Emulsion Medium.

Here a student experiments with overlapping tissues to create a transparent effect.

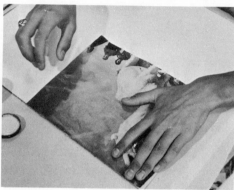

Making a Collage from Magazine Illustrations

1. On a support of thin Masonite with a Gesso ground, the student applies a coat of Polymer Emulsion Medium for affixing a cut-out element.

2. The magazine cut-out is carefully positioned. It is best to affix the top edge first, slowly smoothing down the remainder of the cut-out.

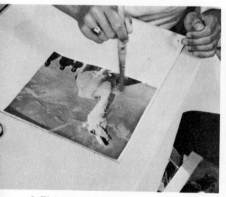

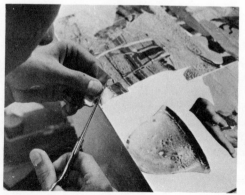

3. The cut-out is brushed with a protective coat of Polymer Emulsion Medium.

4. Other cut-out elements are added to the collage.

5. The finished collage is given a final coat of Polymer Emulsion Medium.

High school student. Collage on chipboard. This complex, richly patterned collage includes magazine cut-outs and photographs. Acrylic Polymer paint was used to create opaque and transparent areas. Final details were drawn in with a fine pen and India ink.

FROTTAGE

Frottage is a technique using drawn or painted patterns which are cut into various shapes and adhered to a support. The object of this procedure is to create a composition using component parts. It provides a fine lesson in learning to compose a picture through rearrangement of design. Pieces of paper are glued to a support in a style which may be rendered realistically or nonobjectively.

The arbitrary use of materials in rebellion against existing styles in art led, in our time, to the development of many unusual techniques. Perhaps this technique is not so ridiculous in retrospect as those of some other periods.

A typical frottage is made in the following way:

1. With a pen or brush, and black ink or Polymer Emulsion paint, make a variety of patterns on an absorbent, quick-drying paper such as newsprint. Such techniques as drybrush, stippling, spattering, wash tones, ink lines on wet surfaces, and others may be explored. Sponging, stamp printing with found objects and finger-printing may also be tried.

2. Cut out a piece of white poster board, railroad board, or heavy white vellum no larger than 12 x 18 inches. Tape it at all four corners to a table.

3. Cut out various interesting shapes from the patterns.

4. Place the shapes on the white board to plan an arrangement.

5. Remove the shapes from the support and coat it generously with Polymer Emulsion Medium, either Matte or Gloss.

6. While certain areas are moist, place one of the forms on the paper. Press and smooth the cut-out shape and apply a generous Emulsion coating over it and each succeeding form adhered.

7. When the shapes are all adhered to the support, and are dry to the touch, apply another coat of Polymer Emulsion over the entire composition. Later, apply a coat of the Emulsion to the reverse side of the design.

To continue working on the design, scratch lines into a color glaze with the handle of the brush, always reglazing the surface.

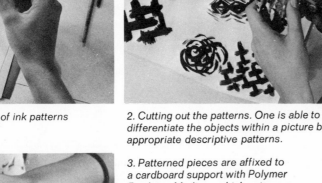

1. Painting a variety of ink patterns with a brush.

2. Cutting out the patterns. One is able to differentiate the objects within a picture by using appropriate descriptive patterns.

3. Patterned pieces are affixed to a cardboard support with Polymer Emulsion Medium, which acts as a binder. Both support and pattern pieces should be coated.

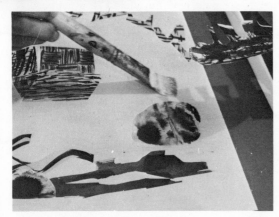

4. Brushing the patterned piece flat onto the support. Polymer Emulsion Medium can also be brushed as a transparent varnish over the cut-out pieces.

5. Patterns will not be affected by the Polymer Emulsion Medium. Detail and color strength, in fact, are preserved by it.

6. The frottage nears completion as the last piece is given a protective varnish with Polymer Emulsion Medium.

Related in concept to the frottage is the *montage*, a design composed of different photographic subjects combined into one picture. These designs are often quite weird as one image is not particularly related to another. Young people love to produce designs which are nonsensical and funny.

The procedure for making a montage is fundamentally the same as that described for the frottage. One may cut out complete photographic images or scour magazines for attractive colors in order to produce a paper mosaic from cut-out shapes. Montages are inexpensive, yet of importance in making a student more aware of composition and color value—and they are a lot of fun to make.

TEXTILE COLLAGE

Artists exploring the many creative possibilities of collage have turned to using textiles with the Polymer Emulsion media. Below are some ways of doing this:

1. Torn and cut textile shapes are affixed to a wet canvas heavily coated with Polymer Gesso. Both transparent and opaque applications of color glazes are brushed over, wiped, and re-applied.

2. Cheesecloth may be adhered to a surface with Polymer Emulsion Medium over which both coarse and fine fabrics such as burlap and muslin may be applied for added richness.

3. One may develop an interesting linear interplay between ground and applied materials. A panel of Masonite coated with a mixture of Polymer Modeling Paste and Polymer Gesso applied thickly would suffice. Once the paste-and-emulsion ground is applied, a large-toothed comb is pulled through it. When the ground is dry, corrugated cardboard shapes are adhered as projections while low-lying shapes may be scraped away.

4. Pliable fabric such as soft cotton, facial tissue, and paper towel pulp may be affixed to a support. A heavy Gesso coat is applied into which the above materials are placed. Another generous Gesso coating is applied over and into the fibrous additives after which they may be manipulated and moved about in order to establish an interesting linear pattern.

Further enhancement of these surfaces can be achieved with glazes, drybrush, or opaque techniques with Polymer Emulsion color.

There are four ways in which to embellish a surface: by additive materials, by carving or incising lines into the surface, by using inherently textural materials for building surfaces, and by painting.

Additives can be applied to a painting support directly into a coating of Polymer Gesso. They are then covered with the same Gesso to become encased with the Polymer film. Facial tissue, pulp tissue, textiles, and string are often incorporated with the ground this way. Fine granular particles may be mixed into the Gesso, but if sawdust is used, it should be pre-saturated thoroughly with Polymer Emulsion Medium because of its absorbent nature. Polymer Modeling Paste may be mixed with Gesso to make a support surface even more textural.

Three-dimensional form may be embellished several ways: by painting, by additive materials, by carving, and by modeling with inherently textural materials. Painting will enhance a smooth clay surface. It also will add variety to high level areas of a rough clay surface; an interplay in light and tone is seen between both the high and low lying areas of the surface. Papier mâché sculpture may be aesthetically enhanced by the application of six or more coats of Polymer Gesso. Glazing may either intensify or mute a color, and such techniques as stippling, scumbling, and spattering are all legitimate methods of applying decoration in color.

Painting techniques help differentiate areas on a relief carving. The incising of lines and carved textural patterns may be complemented by either transparent or opaque Polymer Emulsion color.

The use of additive materials contributes three-dimensionality to a surface. The Modeling Paste, easiest to apply, may be composed of Polymer Emulsion Medium and an inert additive such as Celite, or it may be purchased in the formulated mixture. Painting techniques may be employed to control or to further the effect of the variegated surface.

Students, despite what has been said above, should be aware that the total effect of the sculptural form can be impaired by added color. On the other hand, the materials are themselves interesting in color. Asbestos, sand, and Modeling Paste offer sufficient color for a finished form.

The versatility of the Polymer Emulsion media enables one to use them many ways as embellishment either in one technique, or in combination with others.

PAINTING SUPPORTS

The way a painting support is prepared will affect the eventual results of the embellishment techniques. The Polymer Emulsion media offer the advantages of interesting surface patterns and rapid drying.

Polymer Gesso may be applied flatly and smoothly, in one to six coats, on any kind of support. The inherent texture created by brush markings may be controlled with the fingers by smoothing such marks down. Paper may be incorporated directly into a generous coating of Gesso, over which another coating is applied to encase the additive. If one desires more noticeable surface modulations, such additives as Perltex, Perlite, Zonolite, pumice, marble dust, or sand may be mixed with the Gesso—after they have been

Additives as Surface Embellishment

On a thin Masonite support with a Gesso ground, the student builds up a relief collage of shredded asbestos saturated with Polymer Emulsion Medium.

Further surface ornamentation is produced by adding shallow portions of paper tubes and tissue paper liberally soaked with Polymer Emulsion Medium.

To finish the panel prior to the application of Polymer Emulsion color, small chips of paper or cardboard are fixed in place with white emulsion glue.

saturated in Polymer Emulsion Medium to counteract excess absorption—for direct application to the support. Projections constructed of pieces of cardboard, thin wood, carved Modeling Paste, pieces of glass, and fibrous materials will enliven the normal flatness of the painting surface. Even paper tubes have been adhered to a stiff support with the aid of facial tissue and Polymer Emulsion Medium. Glazes and opaque applications of color may be used to control the effect of the additive materials.

Applications of Gesso are scratched, combed, raked and manipulated in any way to vary the surface. Canvas is naturally textured, but the surfaces of Masonite, Upsom board, and plywood must be altered to provide a more interesting, varied surface on which to work.

A design made with incised lines scratched into a layer of Modeling Paste ⅛ to ¼ inch thick is reminiscent of wall designs found in prehistoric caves. A palette knife, spatula, trowel, putty knife, or table knife may be used to spread a paste mixture on the support. Canvas, in this case, should not be used, as it is too flexible.

One need not be limited to a drawing point in making incisions to define forms. Corrugated cardboard, bottle caps—all manner of odds and ends—may be used as "tools" to make interesting indentations and patterns in a thick ground. Patterns which are deep enough might become wells for applications of glaze. A watercolor mixture or glaze may be wiped away leaving both interesting color tints and heavier notes of color in the incised areas.

As we have seen, a mixture of Polymer Emulsion Medium and color may be extruded from a plastic squeeze bottle into the incised lines. Opaque color combined with transparent glazes provides a richness and depth not possible with thin glazes alone.

Modeling Paste enables one to create a three-dimensional surface akin to low relief as depressed shapes are further scraped away to relate to the projective ones. Color may be used to affect the actual depth afforded by the depressed and raised shapes.

Modeling Paste (or Gesso with added thickeners) can be used to build up a textured surface.

PICTURE FRAMES

Polymer Emulsion Gesso serves admirably as a means of providing surface embellishment, as well as a seal and size, when applied to picture frames in several generous coats. A smooth surface is achieved when sanding is done between coats of Gesso. For a tactile surface, however, use thickeners in the Gesso, apply Modeling Paste thickly to the frame, or glue cutout shapes to the frame's surface. Modeling Paste spread on a frame can be carved or incised when dry to provide decorative motifs. A Paste-and-Gel mixture may be manipulated while it is still moist; or extrusions may be applied with a plastic squeeze bottle. A glaze will further enhance the physical changes made on the flat surface.

Frames having a concave surface are nicely supplemented by further surface treatment. A comb pulled across a layer of Modeling Paste leaves a pleasingly uniform surface treatment. An insert within the larger frame may also be treated with Gesso and textured to complement the frame. Linen or cloth of a heavy basket-weave pattern is recommended for decorating the inner frame.

A comb is pulled through the Modeling Paste to produce a surface texture.

Frames can also be decorated by adhering small pieces of wood or other materials to the surface with white emulsion glue (such as Elmer's Glue-all).

Scooping out Modeling Paste onto a glass palette.

Modeling Paste is applied to the frame with a palette knife.

A relief design can be worked into the damp Modeling Paste with a wooden brush handle . . . or any "handy tool" available.

A strip frame is sometimes preferred by artists and students because of its unobtrusive simplicity. Canvas stretched on four stretcher bars provides a ready-made edge on which to attach such stripping. If Masonite is used for a painting, "one-by-two" fir and redwood strips should be glued to the back of a firm support, as these will not readily warp. This is done by attaching the strips to the perimeter of a support with white Polymer Emulsion glue and small C-clamps or by simply placing bricks or other weights on the strips with the surface to be painted face down. Cross-braces, mitered and glued inside the perimeter strips, should insure against warpage.

The strips for framing should be gessoed and sanded several times prior to the application of color.

Another method uses a wooden frame composed of one-by-four-inch planks joined with mitered edges as a precaution against warping. This is ¼ to ½ inch wider than the support and attached to the back. Lattice stripping is then nailed and glued to this frame so that the thin edge is seen from the front. Again, the recessed area around the support is darkened with color. The advantage of this method lies in the fact that the back frame doubles both as frame and brace for the support.

Strip frames require no embellishment other than Gesso, opaque color, and glaze. However, one may scratch the Gesso and indent the outside surface of the strip prior to coloring it.

Unusual Decoration Techniques

Extrusion techniques are very successfully used to enhance the surface of a frame. The addition of

Gel and perhaps Polymer Emulsion Modeling Paste or some other inert additive material will thicken the Medium to prevent the leveling tendency of the extruded line. Plastic squeeze bottles are excellent for extruding purposes. Recessed flat areas of a frame which lie parallel to the painting surface are ideal places for this treatment.

String dipped into full strength colored Gesso may also be applied to large frame areas if the color tone is too monotonous. Gesso should be adhered to Gesso; thus, apply the Gesso-covered string only to a white or color-toned Gesso surface.

Pre-cast Polymer Emulsion Medium shapes which have set and hardened are very good decorative additive forms.

Embellishment of a surface may also be functional. Polymer Emulsion media may be used to emulate building materials, shrubbery, and landscaping accurately in scale for architectural model making—a popular activity in intermediate and secondary classrooms. (See Part I, Chapter 5.) Their adhesiveness and surface protective qualities make them unique—added to the fact that they are water-base mixtures. Grass is made by coating a panel with a generous application of either the Polymer Emulsion or Gel Medium, and then sprinkling fine sawdust into it. Modeling Paste mixed with green or other emulsion colors may be combed or scratched to look like fields, plowed ground, river banks, etc. Pieces of sponge may be painted to resemble foliage and shrubbery. String dipped into Modeling Paste suffices for figures or small trees. Sawdust mixed with the Gel Medium, carved Modeling Paste, or fluid Modeling Paste is applied as a veneer over papier mâché to provide rough terrain. To build with the Polymer Emulsion media, Modeling Paste is used to make both bricks and foundations, and colored accordingly.

COLOR AND THREE DIMENSIONS

Polymer Emulsion paint, because of its adhesiveness, is ideal for the decoration of models, toys, carvings, modeled forms, ceramics, and puppets. The quick-drying characteristic enables students to proceed more rapidly. In the classroom this advantage benefits storage of constructions which are still wet. Most important is the fact that a varnished exterior is accomplished simply by adding the Polymer Emulsion Medium right into the color. This two-in-one process provides a tougher film than shellac and is done without the need of toxic solvents for thinning or cleaning up.

Full strength color is recommended, but Polymer Emulsion colors may be diluted by as much as three parts water to one part color.

PUPPET HEADS

Once a puppet head has been constructed, it is ready for decoration. A student may want to provide a puppet head with texture to create a greater tactile "naturalism." Crushed egg shells, sawdust, or any granular additive may be sprinkled on while the surface is still wet to make eyebrows, beards, wrinkles, etc. Sawdust is extremely absorbent, but by presaturating it with Polymer Emulsion Medium, bonding is assured.

TOYS

Plastic toys are inert materials—their surfaces do not absorb liquid. The Polymer Emulsion media, however, can be used on plastic, metal, or glass. This is not possible with tempera or any traditional water-base paint. Polymer Emulsion Medium films may flake off inert surfaces if they are not applied completely around the piece being decorated. Even if color is applied only in certain places, the entire surface should be coated with the transparent Polymer Emulsion Medium. Washing of Polymer-coated, hard, impervious surfaces such as plastic, metal, or glass can cause the Polymer to release and peel off.

Decorating a model plane with Acrylic Polymer paints.

GLASS CHIMES

Brass is used in the Orient and Near East for hanging chimes which produce musical, tinkling sounds. Thin pieces of glass may be substituted for this purpose. Heavy duty glass is too heavy, but scraps of window glass, one inch wide, are fine.

A glass cutter will cut long, one-inch strips into lengths of from three to six inches. Differing lengths offer visual interest and, like stringed instruments, produce different tones. Once the short strips are cut they are fixed for hanging by cutting widths of colored cellophane tape or electrical plastic tape in half to bind two pieces of glass of the same size together, sandwiching the heavy thread by which they will be suspended.

Binding the glass is done after decoration is completed on and between the glass. Small pieces of colored tissue are laid into a layer of clear Polymer Emulsion Medium on one of the pieces of glass. Too much tissue will dull the ringing tones. Transparent or opaque lines or shapes in Polymer Emulsion color enhance the tissue. To finish, a fairly generous coat of Polymer Emulsion Medium is painted over the tissue and color, the hanging thread is secured, and a matching piece of glass is placed over the first one. The strips of tape are then bent around both top and bottom of the glued pieces of glass. The exterior of the glass may be further embellished with Polymer Emulsion Medium and color. When eight to twelve or more of these glass constructions are completed, they are attached to a spiraling line of wire and hung from the ceiling. The tinkling results when they are stirred into contact by the slightest breeze.

GLAZING CERAMICS

A ceramic glaze is a hard, vitreous coating applied for protection and decoration. In order for the component minerals that make up the glaze to be transformed from a liquid consistency to a vitreous coating, they must be fired in a kiln at very high temperatures. Carefully worked pieces will often break or suffer some damage in firing. Students can achieve color glazes with the Polymer Emulsion Medium, which does not require heat treatment. This is applied on bisque ware—fired clay which is unglazed.

Transparent Polymer Emulsion Medium mixed with Polymer Emulsion colors has enough gloss to resemble glaze. If more gloss is desired, the painted piece may be coated again with the Polymer Emulsion Gloss Medium.

Sponging, stippling, and scumbling techniques in Polymer Emulsion or Gel Medium add texture and pattern to the clay piece and are applied as in painting. String dipped in Polymer Emulsion Medium, and granular additives, may be glued to its surface for added texture in a coating of Polymer Emulsion color over which transparent glaze is applied. Besides these techniques, the student may explore other ways of incorporating ceramic techniques.

THE PHYSICAL ASPECT OF THE SCULPTURAL SURFACE

Sculpture, being an actual three-dimensional form, brings most of our senses into play through perception alone. When one sees a three-dimensional form, automatically size, weight, color, surface and material, as well as subject, are "felt." Young people are particularly conscious of the "feel" of things, and experiences in producing three-dimensional creations are important activities for them.

Surface decoration of sculpture is achieved in several ways. It may be applied to a completed form or it may be an inherent part of the material of which the form is made. Decorative lines incised on the surface enable the student to delineate his masses as well as avoid monotony in a relief carving without detracting from the form. Polymer Modeling Paste may be used as a smooth coating over a rough inner mass as wax is used over a clay core in bronze casting. Applied in reverse, an interesting rough exterior is achieved.

Asbestos combined with Polymer Emulsion or Gel Medium is a method of making sculpture in which the texture of the component materials also adds to its decorative scheme.

Glazes of thin transparent color may be used as a supplement to a previous glaze on the structure to brighten or dull the effect. Scumbling or dry brushing thickened Polymer color can create interesting tones if tastefully done.

Decorating a ceramic piece with Acrylic Polymer paints.

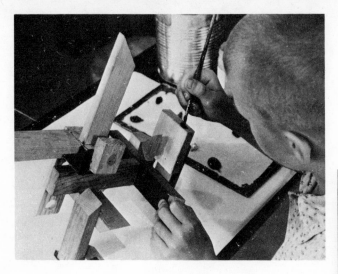

Embellishing an
abstract sculpture
with Acrylic Polymer paints.

Surface Embellishment
of Sculpture

A sculpture form, made of newspaper bound together
with string over a bottle and old light bulb, is decorated
with Acrylic paints.

Because the Acrylic Polymer paints are fast drying, one
may proceed rapidly to the finishing touches.

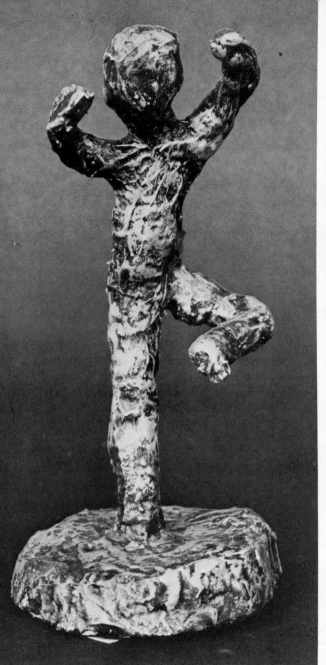

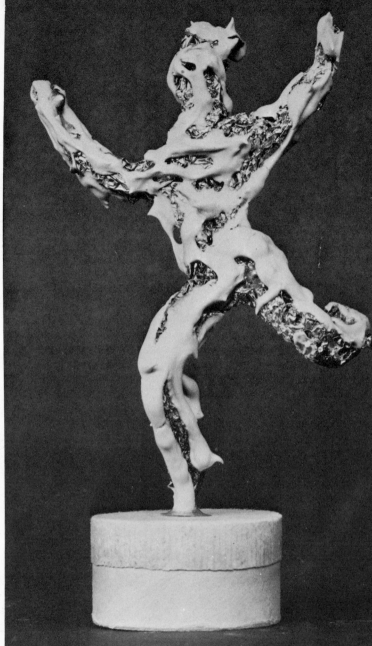

Modeling Paste enhances the surface of this figure made of Pariscraft.

A running figure of aluminum foil is decorated with a thick, bold application of Modeling Paste.

Print making is a graphic process which enables one to mechanically reproduce the same design more than once. There are four basic print making methods: relief, intaglio, planographic, and stenciling. **Relief** (or letterpress) printing is done from a relief created by carving into a surface or gluing additive lines or planes to it. **Intaglio** refers to the act of incising or scratching; with this method, prints are produced by ink pulled from areas which lie below the surface of the plate. The **planographic** process (the principle of lithography) is a resist method and the only process impossible to reproduce with Polymers. **Stenciling** (or silk screen printing) is a method of printing through a fine mesh to produce a design; the areas not to be printed are stopped out with glue or shellac.

Oil-base printer's ink is used by most artists and students, although some prefer the water-soluble inks.

While Polymer Emulsion media are not recommended as printing inks for some graphic processes (the adhesiveness of the Polymer Emulsion would make the customary wiping for intaglio printing rather difficult), they may be used satisfactorily in relief and simple stencil printing techniques. In addition, Polymer paints may be used for silk screen colors, and the Medium serves admirably as a stopout for a silk screen itself.

RELIEF PRINTING

Relief prints are accomplished by two general methods: stamp printing and block printing. Potato stamp printing is an ideal technique for use in school, especially in the lower grades. Other simple tools would include the edges of cardboard, the ends of rolled paper, carved erasers, and found objects such as spools, bottle caps, and the like.

Using glass as a palette, Polymer Emulsion color from jars or tubes may be thinned with a little water for stamp printing. The richness of color is retained despite dilution. Newsprint, easel paper, thin white bond, colored tissue, and construction paper may serve as printing paper. The absorbency of the paper and the rapid drying of the paint are definite advantages for the teacher concerned about easy storage.

A more sophisticated procedure, block printing, is of greater interest to the young adult. His manipulative skills, perceptual awareness of reality, and physical strength enable him to do more intricate things in art. He should be encouraged to explore various ways to make a print. The following are some approaches to the block printing techniques.

Relief printing by synthesis. One can produce a very effective line by dipping a piece of string into Polymer Emulsion Medium and placing it on a block of chipboard or wood which has been prepared with a generous coat of Medium. By adding such materials as cardboard, innertube, buttons, etc., one may supplement the string for a more complex design. These materials are adhered to the printing surface with Polymer Emulsion Medium or white glue. Then a protective coat of Polymer Emulsion Medium is brushed over the entire surface. Ink with a brayer rolled through a viscous mixture of Polymer Emulsion Medium and color on a sheet of glass. If the color

Corrugated Paper makes a Relief Plate

After the initial planning stage, any available tool may be used by the small child to cut away the soft top layer of corrugated paper for a simple relief pattern. The inner grooves add extra ready-made interest and other areas may be simply cut through and discarded. A coating of Polymer Emulsion Medium brushed over the "plate" will strengthen it before applying color with a brayer.

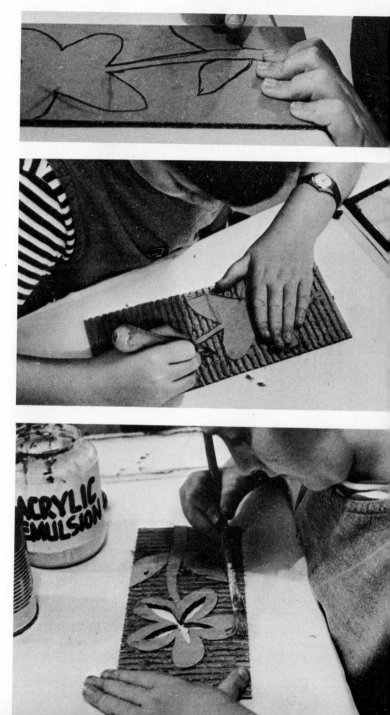

starts to set on the glass, sprinkle a little water on the mixture. For more professional results, it is advisable to pre-wet the printing paper, and then blot it between sheets of newspaper before printing. Inexpensive pre-cut rice paper is the best stock one can use for printing. Hang the prints to dry on a clothesline.

Extrusion relief lines are interesting to print from and students will be fascinated by being able to draw lines without pencil, pen or brush. A plastic squeeze bottle is filled to one third capacity with Polymer Emulsion Medium mixed with two parts color, to which a one fifth part thickener, such as wheat paste, powdered clay, or spackling compound, is added. Tubed Polymer Emulsion paints can be squeezed directly onto the surface or used in a plastic squeeze bottle to produce a raised line which will not level.

If leveling of extruded color occurs, it may be compensated for by sprinkling fine sand or Perltex on the extruded lines as they harden. Upon drying, Polymer Emulsion Medium should be brushed over the extrusions to protect the raised line as well as the particles. The extrusions should be allowed to dry from four hours to overnight; concentrated Polymer Emulsion Medium congeals in minutes, but a longer time is required for complete drying. Printing paper is laid over the raised lines and an inked brayer is then lightly rolled over it.

POLYMER MODELING PASTE RELIEF

Polymer Modeling Paste may be used to make a relief printing block. There are definite advantages to be gained from using Modeling Paste: mistakes may be covered up, and textural qualities occur which can contribute a uniqueness to the final product. One block can be used to make many different prints just by reapplying and recutting the paste.

A relief design is drawn with the Polymer Gel Medium on paper; when thoroughly dry it is inked with a brayer and rolled through the wringer to print.

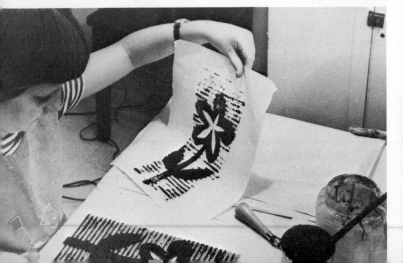

Stamp Printing with Found Objects

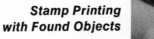

Potatoes, erasers, bottle caps, sponges and other found objects are satisfactory forms to be carved or used as found for stamping on paper or fabric employing Acrylic Polymer colors thinned with a little water.

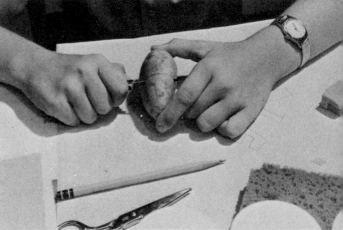

After a piece of plywood or Masonite or a square of vinyl floor tile is selected for the printing block, four or five thin layers of Modeling Paste are troweled onto the block with a palette knife. Each coat should dry before another is applied. The layers should be no more than ¼ inch thick or serious cracking may result. Smooth down the last coat with a wood file. Small gouges, linoleum cutters, knives, burins, and even nails may be used for cutting the design.

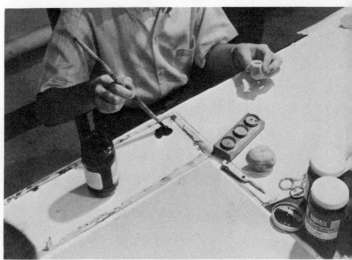

A block print in low relief is obtained by drawing the design on paper with thickened Polymer Gel Medium. After drying it is inked and printed in the manner of an ordinary block print.

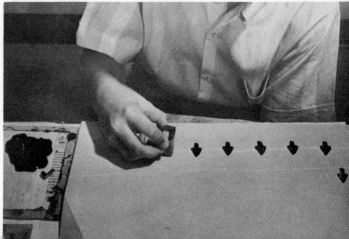

Chipboard or thin wood coated with a generous layer of Polymer Emulsion Medium functions as a support for cut-out patterns which will adhere to the Emulsion. String dipped into Emulsion enhances the design. The Acrylic Polymer Emulsion color for printing should be viscous and applied with a brayer from a glass sheet palette.

Relief Printing Block of Polymer Modeling Paste

Any slips or errors in transferring the design to the block are easily repaired using the Polymer media.

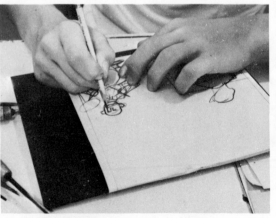

Creating the original design.

Cutting the plywood base to fit.

Using the palette knife to apply thin ¼" layers of Polymer Modeling Paste which are allowed to dry between each application.

When desired depth is reached the final coat is sanded smooth with a wood file.

Gouging away this soft surface is effortless and a slip is corrected with some Modeling Paste added to the injured area. No other block print method has this advantage.

Roll the brayer in ink and print with normal spooning process.

Monoprinting is easily accomplished with the Polymer Emulsion colors. After wetting and blotting a sheet of paper, it is placed over a still wet, painted design, which has been rendered on a sheet of glass. Using register marks in order that the corners of the paper may be repositioned over the same area, one may repaint the area and print several overlapping designs to get a print of unexpected richness and depth. Pieces of colored paper or textile can be glued to the printing paper to vary the results. Because of their versatility and the ease with which the Polymer media are used, one might try printing transparent colors over opaque ones for tonal variety and applying transparent glazes between the overlapping and overprinted designs.

INTAGLIO PRINTING

Polymer Emulsion media enable one to accomplish intaglio techniques in the simplest, safest, and most direct way. An untempered Masonite block, eight by ten inches, beveled at the edges, is given about six coats of Gesso and sanded smooth. Then about six coats of Matte Polymer Emulsion Medium are applied evenly. Brush marks can be eliminated by thinning the Medium with water. When the Medium is set, after about an hour, etch the surface by using a simple woodburning tool. Mistakes are easily repainted with the Emulsion Medium. As the woodburning tool becomes coated with the Medium, lacquer thinner or Polymer Emulsion Remover can be used to clean it.

A variety of lines is possible with a woodburning tool which has interchangeable tips.

To print, the synthetic plate is carefully heated and inked with a dauber. Tarletan, or some crinolines, can be used to wipe away excess ink which has not been forced into the incisions. Good quality cold press drawing paper (over forty-pound is recommended) or watercolor stock which has been pre-moistened and blotted is placed over the inked surface. A blanket of felt, ⅛ inch thick, is folded around the plate and paper, and then rolled through the press. A washer wringer will serve the purpose. Oil paint may be used as printing ink in low budget situations.

Polymer Emulsion as a Printing Ink

88

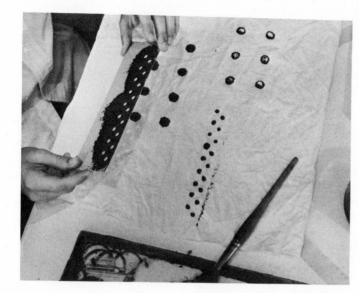

Simple stencil designs are developed for fabric decoration using punched holes in cardboard, brushed over with thinned quick-drying polymer paints. Combining the stamping and stenciling techniques offers a greater color and design experience.

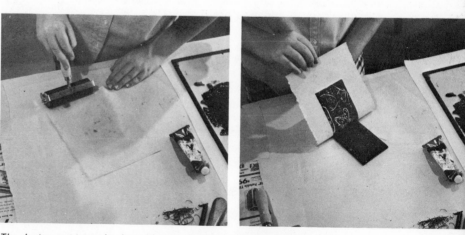

The design, cut into a linoleum block, is inked with Acrylic Polymer color which is spread on a glass palette directly from the tube. Pre-cut rice paper is inexpensive and, pressed to the block, results in a very satisfactory print.

COLLAGRAPHY

Derived from collage, collagraphy, a new print-making technique, has recently become popular. Many materials have been used for this process from sawdust and string on cardboard covered with Gesso to the synthetic epoxy metals applied to thin metal plates. This print-making method is identical with the intaglio process except for additive materials. These additives—lithography grinding powders, fine sand, paper, cardboard, cheesecloth, pelon, textiles, and other things—are incorporated into the Polymer Emulsion Medium. Fibrous additives are placed into a wet coating of Medium and brushed over with another coating. Granular additives are first mixed with the Polymer Emulsion Medium in a container and are then applied to the surface with a palette knife or heavy brush. Polymer Modeling Paste may be added to the pre-affixed additives as a complementary shape or textured area. At least two coats of Emulsion Medium are finally applied over the entire surface. Incised lines add linear relief to the textured shapes. Too great an inconsistency in the use of heavy and thin additives must be avoided, otherwise a sensitive design will not reproduce evenly.

OTHER CONSIDERATIONS

Old metal plates, if available, may be used as printing supports, as the Polymer Emulsion Medium will fill in any old incisions. It must be remembered that the Medium should completely encompass the non-porous metal surface, as moisture on any bare metal area may cause the film to peel.

An apron is necessary in any printing procedure. Polymer Emulsion media, because of their adhesive strength, particularly necessitate the use of one.

If a great deal of subtlety is desired, one may use a technique related to those already discussed. A small sheet of Plexiglas—also a Polymer product—may be used as a printing support into which lines are burned directly. To this may be added, however, some Gel Medium which is brushed on in certain places to be scratched, brushed, or textured. The Gel Medium may also be pre-cast on glass in wells formed by oil-base clay, and later glued to the plastic sheet. String or thread may be dipped into Polymer Emulsion Medium and laid in linear patterns on the Plexiglas surface to relate to the incised lines.

Students should be encouraged to explore innovations. Separate blocks of glass, Masonite, wood, metal, or plastic might be used for the printing of different component shapes to make one complete print. The same print would then have to be repeatedly rolled through the press because of the number of different shapes involved. Both relief and intaglio methods could be combined in this process.

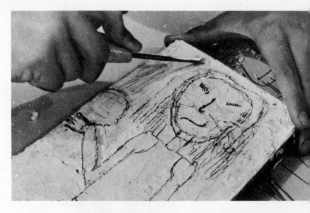

Relief sculpture carved into a surface built up of several layers of Polymer Modeling Paste on a Masonite support.

Sculpture falls into three basic types: relief, in the round, and construction. Sculpture may be made by modeling, carving, and building techniques, with a great variety of materials. Among the newest, most reliable and malleable of these are the Polymer Emulsion media. Weight, composition, texture, color and materials are of interest to the student acquiring knowledge daily from the handling of the three-dimensional mass.

RELIEF TECHNIQUES

Relief, frequently carved in plaster of Paris, is easily done with Polymer Modeling Paste. The time required to prepare a block for carving is more than compensated for by the ease of carving and strength of material. Plaster of Paris is a fragile and brittle material which will crack and chip very easily. Polymer Modeling Paste allows the beginner to carve lines, define shapes, and establish textural patterns with linoleum tools, wood carving tools, scribers, and even carpenter's nails. In addition, the tough film provided by Polymer Emulsion in combination with additives in the Paste prevents accidental dents from impairing the design.

Preparing a block for relief carving is the same as in block printing (See Part II, Chapter 8). A block of plywood, piece of Masonite of ⅛ inch thickness, a vinyl floor tile, or Upsom board is given about four applications of Modeling Paste. Polymer Emulsion Medium is mixed with the Modeling Paste to provide strength, elasticity, and ease of handling. The individual Paste layers should not be more than ¼ inch in thickness, as cracking is likely to occur due to the shrinkage caused by too rapid a rate of water evaporation as it dries.

For greater economy the Polymer Modeling Paste is applied over a figure of aluminum foil pressed upon a wire armature.

These figures are sculptured of pure Polymer Modeling Paste.

RELIEF BY SYNTHESIS

A collage technique using pre-cut materials and found objects for design components provides an interesting sculpturing experience. Such materials would include blocks of wood, bottle caps, cardboard, and tissue manipulated into ridges by a brush. An easy way to build shapes is to begin by dipping string into Gesso and placing it on a panel. Odd textures are produced by sprinkling additives into wet Gesso in certain areas. For variety, however, one need go no further than using textiles to create patterns for needed interest.

Further decoration is done in conventional ways—carving lines, digging patterns, scratching through one paint layer to expose another, and using transparent glazes.

IN THE ROUND

Perhaps the most direct method of making sculpture in the round is with the Polymer Modeling Paste.

Open a can of Modeling Paste, remove a portion of the Paste, and allow the water to evaporate from it until it reaches the consistency of modeling clay. Gel Medium is then worked into the Paste in a ratio of one part Gel to two parts Paste. This will prevent cracking. The mixture may then be modeled with the hands. After the modeled piece has been allowed to set for a day it may be carved with a cutting tool. About four or five days later it may be chiseled, filed, sanded and buffed. Buffing and polishing bring out the true character of the marble dust, one of the main ingredients of the Paste. The form will have enough elasticity to be protected even if it falls to the floor.

If one desires color, Polymer Emulsion paint may be incorporated with the modeling medium. Transparent glazes of the Polymer Emulsion Medium, and gold gilding medium, may be applied to achieve special effects. Emulsion colors are applied quickly with Polymer Emulsion or Gel Medium, and these are further protected by either Polymer Emulsion Gloss, or Matte Varnish. The Polymer Emulsion media enable one to make alterations quickly, are unaffected by damage which could affect shellac, are impervious to moisture, and they do not show the change of color tone so typical of tempera when it dries.

Students and beginners will find excitement with this new modeling medium. However, when economy is a factor, an armature of wire and aluminum foil, papier mâché, or a clay base will cut down the need to make the piece entirely from Modeling Paste. An outer shell of the Modeling Paste is sufficient.

Papier mâché can be made with the Polymer Emulsion Medium in much the same way it is with traditional media. Newspaper or paper toweling is soaked overnight in water. Then the water is drained off and Polymer Emulsion Medium is added. A test piece should be made to prove that enough Polymer Medium has been used in order that structural strength is assured.

Small pieces of paper are easier to manipulate, but if one is to produce an ambitious form, larger paper sheets will be easier to apply to the surface. A large form should have a chicken wire support or an armature of wood built up with large amounts of paper tied to the frame. Styrofoam or wood may be used, but several liberal coats of Polymer Emulsion Medium over the surface are necessary. Interweaving the papier mâché in strips is recommended for covering a large mass, while a mulch of shredded paper suffices for detail.

For speed, one might use an armature of styrofoam. It is easily cut and shaped into a form over which the Modeling Paste is troweled and manipulated.

It is also possible to produce an adequate armature by mixing one half Polymer Emulsion Medium and one half water with shredded paper, sawdust, Perlite and Vermiculite. This is shaped and allowed to dry before the Paste is applied. New layers of Modeling Paste may be added at any time to build up the existing form. Pre-wetting the form before applying the new Paste mixture is essential to avoid having the existing form absorb too much binder from the new mixture. If absorption does occur, the new layer is apt to crack.

MODELING AND TEXTURE

Various additive materials such as asbestos, sawdust, and sand may be used to enhance the tactile quality of the sculptured surface. They are incorporated by sprinkling, brushing, or patting them into a very wet surface.

Asbestos saturated with Polymer Emulsion Medium is a very satisfactory modeling material for the classroom.

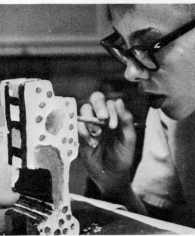

The Polymer Emulsion Medium seals the pores of a carved plaster block so it may be decorated with color.

Employing the adhesiveness, color and surface finish of the Polymer media in constructing a relief sculpture.

CONSTRUCTION

Sculpture by construction involves building a single structural whole with a series of planes. In using the Polymer Emulsion Medium one must think of opaque, transparent, and molded surfaces. Opaque surfaces include wood, metal, and even Polymer Emulsion media, or anything which would relate to or could be used with non-transparent planes. When painting designs on metal, remember that if the metal should have a smooth, shiny surface, the entire surface must be thoroughly encased in a film of Polymer Emulsion Medium. The adhesiveness of the Polymer enables it to thoroughly cover any surface, absorbent or non-porous. A non-porous material should have a slight "tooth" or rough surface for the Polymer to adhere permanently.

Transparency in construction has the advantage with the Polymer media of being alternately opaque or clear. Configurations and parts of transparent design may be opaqued to provide visual interest and completeness. Polymer glazes provide interesting color effects applied on glass decorated with colored tissue or to a piece of colored cellophane between two cardboard windows.

The most effective way of utilizing Polymer Emulsion for the emission of light is by molding it. Plastic shapes can be cast within an oil-base clay enclosure, which will harden to a transparent state (See Part 1, Chap. 2, p. 36). Colored glass, plastic beads, etc., may be dropped into the cast plastic before it sets fast. Glass will be transparent but Polymer color settles into a translucent mass.

Wire rings can form enclosures for cast plastic shapes; these then could be incorporated with other designs for a mobile of great beauty.

Exploration with transparents, opaques, or both in combination will reveal even more design possibilities.

THREE-DIMENSIONAL CRAFT USES OF POLYMER EMULSION MEDIA

Three projects immediately come to mind in regard to crafts utilizing the Polymer Emulsion media. They are mask making, puppetry, and jewelry design.

MASKS

The most permanent, sculptural method of making masks involves using a mold. The mold form, which resembles a bas relief, is modeled with clay on a plaster bat. Wood modeling tools are used to define the features. To make the mask, about six layers of wet paper strips are laid over the finished clay form. The paper should be pre-cut and soaked overnight before use. Then about six layers of paper which has been dipped into a pan containing half water and half Polymer Emulsion Medium are placed over the form. Gently press the paper down onto the mold. Finally, this is covered by pieces of white tissue which may be pre-soaked or brushed over with the Medium. After the tissue has completely dried, the clay is removed from the newly formed plastic and paper shell. White tissue is used to seal over any roughness left by the clay. The luminosity of this white surface will brighten the Polymer Emulsion color which is painted over the surface. Granular additives may be sprinkled on a coating of Gel Medium for surface variation. This is done prior to painting the mask.

Extruded Polymer color from a plastic squeeze bottle may also add texture.

PUPPETS

Puppet heads and costumes benefit greatly by the use of the Polymer Emulsion media. Costumes can be printed with Polymer colors pounced through a stencil for repeated motifs. Puppet heads can be modeled in the fashion described above for masks. Small facial protrusions are squeezed into recognizable shape using the soaked tissue or newspaper. Paper is soaked overnight, drained, put into a pan containing a mixture of half water and half Polymer Medium. The pieces are first put on a light bulb or ball of clay. As this is to be removed, no Polymer Emulsion Medium is applied. Six layers of this paper are followed by six layers of paper saturated in the Medium. More Medium-coated paper is applied to the head and squeezed into the necessary features. Paper may be rolled into coils and laid on the surface to become pronounced appendages. These are usually stripped over with more paper for adhesion. Upon drying, the head is slammed against a hard surface to loosen the bulb from the shell of plastic. The bottom of the head, which has been opened for removal of the bulb or clay base, is sealed when the head has been emptied of the mold. In the case of marionettes, a wire hook is installed in the bottom of the head and secured by paper coated with Emulsion Medium. Colors are then used to decorate the head. Hair may be dipped into Polymer Emulsion Medium and laid onto the head for drying. Or a wig of dry yarn is cut and laid on a masking tape strip. This is then attached to the head and Polymer Emulsion Medium is brushed over the tape. A granular additive sprinkled on Gel Medium will also serve as hair.

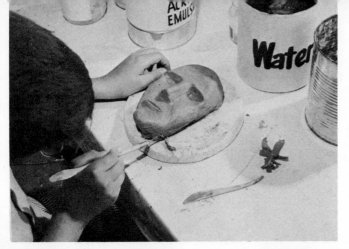

Making a Mask
with Polymers

Polymer Emulsion-soaked paper strips are draped on a clay mold in the familiar papier mâché technique. After removing the clay a white tissue surface covering is glazed with Emulsion and may be decorated with color, additives, and Polymer Gel relief lines pre-mixed and extruded from a plastic squeeze-bottle.

A Lampbulb Puppet Head

Using the same technique as in building the mask, with the exception of applying the first layers with paper strips pre-soaked in plain water as the glass bulb base is to be smashed and removed after the Polymer Emulsion head has set. Short lengths of knitting yarn set on masking tape make the wig, and a paper cone hat covers any unevenness.

When modeling in clay, children are apt to overwork and smooth down the surface. The consistency of Modeling Paste encourages a fresh and texturally rich surface quality as seen in these Pariscraft figures constructed on a base of clay or aluminum foil with a final surface of Polymer Modeling Paste or of Polymer Gel Medium as in the mask.

JEWELRY

Most young people love to make jewelry; however, it is usually left to the secondary school to provide all the experiences students may get in this craft, which is as creative as any.

An easy way to make jewelry is to glue found objects from nature onto a small plane with white glue or to use the Polymer Emulsion media. Nature jewelry is often very fragile; while those pieces made with Polymer media are tough, resilient, and colorful. Painting small, fired clay shapes; casting Polymer Emulsion Medium inside enclosures; and dipping strings into Polymer Emulsion Medium to establish enclosures and to define shapes on a plane are some of the ways this Medium could be used in jewelry making. A piece of styrene plastic from a used container may serve as a ground onto which colored beads, sequins, or other granular substances are glued with Polymer Emulsion.

Beads of fired clay are easy for children to make. They are formed by rolling clay in one's hand until a ball is formed; or they may be squeezed around a stretched line of wire. If nichrome wire is used they may be hung in the kiln for firing. The Polymer Emulsion colors are painted onto the fired clay beads and hung to dry. Polymer Emulsion Medium is then painted over them to protect the color. Watermelon seeds, which make fine necklaces, may be given a protective coating of the plastic. Modeling Paste may be rolled into beads and no firing process is needed. Color may be added to the Paste or the dried beads may be painted.

Clay shapes make attractive pendants. They are easy to model because of the plasticity of the clay, and they are very light in weight after being fired in a kiln, if they are not more than one fourth inch thick. Incised lines may be filled by extruding color into them with a small plastic squeeze bottle. They may be glazed or painted opaquely in the normal way, and objects such as alphabet noodles may be glued on for names or initials. A brooch requires only a small pin glued to the back. These techniques may also be accomplished with air dried Modeling Paste. It is slightly heavier than clay but is much more durable in nature and no kiln is needed for firing.

conclusion

This is an era of quick change, reflected in the sensitive art world. Despite the fact that many artists still prefer using traditional media and techniques, synthetics, used throughout our culture for consumer goods, have been introduced as art media and are fast growing in popularity.

Constant improvement has established the importance and reliability of synthetic media. The new polymerization process, first used in industry, entails the transforming of small molecules into larger ones which join into chains of interlocked, durable and pliable components. This flexibility, retained in many of the forms in which the media are available, emphasizes the advantage of using synthetic media for artistic expression. The addition of certain chemicals and the manufacture of the water-thinned Polymer Emulsions have made these thermoplastic resin vehicles most attractive for executing artistic ideas. Research and reformulations of coal tar dyes produced colors of unequaled quality, durability, and brilliance.

The advantages in using the completely non-toxic Polymer Emulsion media would include:

1. brilliance of hue
2. flexibility, unaffected by the expansion and contraction of a support
3. paint film is strong, durable and damage resistant
4. faster drying of color overlays
5. when dry, paint surface may be washed with water and detergent
6. properly applied, the paint is completely impervious to moisture
7. non-toxic and available in many interactive physical forms
8. used under oil media as an undercoating or imprimatura coating
9. very versatile, it will adapt to various techniques
10. excellent covering power in either matte or gloss
11. easiest medium with which to apply glazes
12. strongest adhesion of any commercially prepared art medium
13. will accept innumerable additives
14. no pre-sizing or final varnish needed
15. no fat-over-lean problem as exists with oil colors
16. may be worked on an almost unlimited variety of supports

The Polymer Emulsion media are excellent for craft work such as puppetry, masks, and jewelry. Sculpture, particularly, may be accomplished in a variety of ways and actually is strengthened by the addition of Polymer coatings, color glazes, etc., in relief, in the round, and in constructions.

Linear, granular, and fibrous additives are easily affixed to a support in painting to enhance the surface. Absorbent additives should be pre-saturated and applied to, or within, the moist media. Extrusion techniques of trailing a Polymer Emulsion mixture of Medium and color, the casting of solid blocks in liquid plastic, and the dipping of materials such as string into either Gesso or the Emulsion Medium for placement on a support are all very easily done with the Polymer Emulsion media. Painting supports may be further embellished with a papier mâché mixture or a layer of Polymer Modeling Paste into which configurations may be rendered.

Transparency is a natural quality of Polymer Emulsion media, and provides endless possibilities of casting shapes. Functional decorative forms such as room dividers, lamp shades, wall hangings, mobiles, stained glass panels, ceramic constructions and jewelry, to mention just a few, all may be accomplished with these versatile, almost incredible media.

The importance of the new Polymer media in the classroom cannot be estimated. The well-balanced school art program necessitates a variety of materials—tempera, watercolor, oil paint, and inks—which are now duplicated by the new aqueous preparations and need no longer be stocked.

The few disadvantages of the new media are negligible; the staining of garments, their rapid drying characteristics, and, under certain circumstances, the tendency for the painting to develop a sticky surface. All can be remedied. Smocks or aprons should be worn, and brush cleaner, lacquer thinner and hot water applied to the area of a stain will loosen the color for removal. The rapidity of drying may be retarded when necessary by repeated spraying with water. There are now some new retarding gels being offered by a few companies. Back-to-front stacking solves the sticking problem caused by storing work in excessively hot areas.

The most important considerations in art classroom situations are versatility, durability, and economy. These are all factors which the Polymer media fully satisfy. The fact that other media may be incorporated is significant. Papier mâché is built inexpensively, and, used with Polymer carvings, is an important experience for older students who may further enhance the construction with Polymer Emulsion colors. Because of the range of the plastic colors, it is possible to decorate mosaic tesserae for use in permanent school murals at a definite saving.

Never-ending research by men like Henry Levison, Leonard Bocour, and Albert Duca will inevitably result in new, improved plastic painting media. The vast improvements made in the last twenty years have laid a solid foundation from which more and better things are likely to build in the area of synthetic media for art. Exploration by student and teacher, artist and layman could indeed make using synthetic media a continuing and more exciting experience.

MATERIALS AND MANUFACTURERS' LIST

Aqua-Tec (acrylic polymer emulsion artist's media)................Bocour Artists Colors, Inc.
552 West 52 Street
New York 19, N. Y.
(and art supply stores)

Carborundum (hard, black abrasive in granular form)...............industrial suppliers

Celite (a type of diatomaceous earth)............................Johns-Manville, Inc.
Sales Corp.
270 Madison Avenue
New York, N. Y.
(and through large paint and
building suppliers)

Hyplar (copolymer emulsion artist's media)........................M. Grumbacher, Inc.
460 West 34 Street
New York, N. Y.
(and art supply stores)

Inert additives (clays, Celite, pumice, silica, talc, whiting)............E. Ferzandie and Sperrle, Inc.
103 Lafayette Street
New York, N. Y.
(and pigment and building
suppliers)

Liquitex (acrylic polymer emulsion artist's media)...................Permanent Pigments, Inc.
2700 Highland Avenue
Norwood, Ohio
(and art supply stores)

New Masters (copolymer emulsion paint for artists).................California Products, Corp.
169 Waverly Street
Cambridge 39, Mass.
(and art supply stores)

Pelon (a fibrous, reinforcement cloth for garments)................department stores

Perlite (expanded mica, granular additive for building materials).......building suppliers

Perltex (sand float for paint, pulverized volcanic ash)...............Western Mineral Products, Inc.
4725 Olson Highway
Minneapolis 22, Minnesota
(and paint suppliers)

Plexiglas (acrylic plastic sheeting)................................building suppliers

Polymer Tempera (polyvinyl acetate emulsion).....................for formula, write:
The Borden Chemical Co.
Foster Street
Peabody, Mass.

Shiva Acrylic (acrylic polymer emulsion media for artists)...........Shiva Artist Colors
Shiva-Rhodes Building
Tenth and Monroe Streets
Paducah, Kentucky

Spackling compound (plaster-like compound for patching)...........paint and hardware stores

Styrofoam (a soft polystyrene composition).......................Dow Chemical Co.
Midland, Mich.
(and department stores)

Vermiculite (expanded mica for use as an aggregate
with building materials)......................................building suppliers